A CONCISE HISTORY OF RUSSIA

A CONCISE HISTORY OF

RUSSIA

RONALD HINGLEY

A STUDIO BOOK

THE VIKING PRESS · NEW YORK

To my children

Russia's past has been admirable. Her present is more than magnifi-
cent. As to her future, it is beyond the power of the most daring imagination to portray.

That, my friend, is the point of view from which Russian history
should be conceived and written.

GENERAL COUNT ALEXANDER BENCKENDORFF, *Chief of
Gendarmes and Chief Controller of the Third Section of His Imperial
Majesty's Personal Chancellery under the Emperor Nicholas I*

The stifling emptiness and dumbness of Russian life, curiously
combined with its vitality and rumbustious character, give rise to all
sorts of crackpot outbursts in our midst.

ALEXANDER HERZEN, *political defector*

A Russian takes incredible delight in every kind of scandalous public
upheaval.

THEODORE DOSTOYEVSKY, *novelist and political criminal*

Frontispiece: The Church of the Transfiguration, Kizhi

Copyright © *1972 Thames and Hudson Ltd London*

Published in 1972 by The Viking Press, Inc.
625 Madison Avenue, New York, N.Y. 10022

SBN *670 23651 9*

Library of Congress catalog card number: 77-157971 3·10·72
Printed and bound in Great Britain by Jarrold and Sons Ltd, Norwich

Contents

Preface

The more concise a historical study is, the more conscious its author must be that his every page could be qualified or challenged by reference to scores of different sources and authorities. Yet the very demands of conciseness must deter him from plaguing his readers with repeated caveats, reservations and complaints about the difficulty of doing justice to complex events in a minimum of words. May this single lamentation therefore suffice to emphasize once and for all my respect for the eternal elusiveness of historical truth? I also hope that it will excuse any air of undue briskness in disposing of knotty controversies which deserve more space than they have received.

Among the numerous major topics (political, social, dynastic, economic, military, religious and so on) which a concise historian of Russia must attempt to cover, one in particular – the cultural – seems to lend itself less to condensed treatment than any other. To have attempted more than a glancing description of phenomena as complex as Russian literature, music, painting and architecture within so brief a compass would have been to risk the glib cliché and the snap generalization in especially ugly juxtaposition. I have therefore decided not to aim at the reader's instruction in this area so much as to remind him of Russia's main cultural achievements in passing, or to invoke them solely in the form of illustrations.

Russian names occurring in the text are transliterated or otherwise rendered along lines laid down at length in the Prefaces to volumes 1–8 of *The Oxford Chekhov*, edited and translated by myself and published by the Oxford University Press. Dates relating to the period between 1 January 1700 and 1 February 1918 accord with the Julian Calendar used in Russia at that time. This means that they lag behind the dates used in western Europe: by thirteen days in the twentieth century, by twelve days in the nineteenth century, and by eleven days in the eighteenth century.

RONALD HINGLEY
Frilford, Abingdon

Chapter One

INTRODUCTION

Modern Russia is an industrial and military super-power dominating the global scene in the middle and later decades of the twentieth century in competition with the United States of America.

Officially known since 1922 as the USSR (Union of Soviet Socialist Republics), Russia covers a sixth of the earth's land surface, being more than twice as large as any other state. The population was recorded as approaching 230,000,000 in 1965, but is not dense by comparison with that of other leading industrial states, or with that of China and India, being especially sparse in Asiatic Russia.

Russia-in-Asia includes the vastness of Siberia, and accounts for about three-quarters of the total area of the USSR, but the country's main historical develop-ments have been firmly based on its European territory – itself large enough to dwarf all other European states. Three capital cities have played an especially potent role. From the ninth to the eleventh centuries AD and beyond, Kiev headed a loose federation of principalities. Then, after a long interval when Russia had no single unchallenged chief city, Moscow became the capital: from the fifteenth century until 1712. The next capital was St Petersburg, later briefly named Petrograd, now Leningrad. In 1918 the seat of government was transferred back to Moscow.

Russia's climate varies from arctic severity in the north to sub-tropical heat in the south, being generally of the extreme continental variety, with excessively severe winters. Four main vegetational belts may be distinguished: tundra in the far north, then forest, then steppe, and finally the deserts of the extreme south. Among these zones only the intermediate forest and steppe have been of central importance in Russian history. With regard to relief, the Russian land mass essen-tially consists of a huge plain ringed only on parts of its southern perimeter, as also in eastern Siberia, by high mountains. Complex river systems form com-munication links vital to internal transport, but ill equipped for international

7

trade since they mainly pour into land-locked or icebound waters (the Arctic Ocean, the Black, the Baltic and the White Seas), including lakes termed seas (the Caspian and the Aral).

Russia is, and has been for several centuries, a state of many nationalities, many languages and many religions, Russians themselves being only the most numerous among over a hundred different peoples. To cater for so varied a population the USSR is divided into fifteen constituent Union Republics, the whole complex being dominated by its largest member – the giant Russian Soviet Federative Socialist Republic (RSFSR), which includes Moscow, Leningrad and all Siberia.

The Russian Empire was united until 1917 by the profession of an official state creed, that of the Orthodox Church, alongside which a variety of other religions also flourished. Owing to the widespread profession of Old Belief (by dissenters from Orthodoxy) and of Protestantism (including a profusion of minor sects) – as also of Catholicism, Judaism, Islam, Buddhism and other faiths – Imperial Russia was a truly multi-religious community. Since 1917 religious practice has been discouraged and persecuted in all its forms, but still struggles on – now in rivalry with the officially imposed secular cult of Marxism-Leninism.

Politically speaking, Russia has been distinguished for over six centuries by authoritarian rule of progressively but erratically increasing severity, generally under a single supreme ruler. These autocrats have included, in chronological order, Mongol Khans, Muscovite Grand Princes, Tsars, Tsar-Emperors (and Tsaritsa-Empresses), as well as several communist dictators or near-dictators. From the fifteenth to the nineteenth century the Russian monarchy grew ever more absolute, its impact being somewhat relaxed from 1855 onwards, and then slightly more relaxed again after 1905. There was a brief period of complete freedom from authoritarian rule between February and October 1917, power being then seized by Bolshevik revolutionaries under Lenin and Trotsky, after which the yet more autocratic regimen of totalitarianism came to replace monarchic absolutism.

Dominant influence within the totalitarian state is exercised by the only per-mitted political party, the Communist Party of the Soviet Union. Originally more élitist, this is now a much expanded organization, but still includes only about four per cent of the population, and is itself severely hierarchical in the sense that policy is dictated from the top, not formed at 'grass roots' level. The party – and in effect a small leading group or an individual leader – is deemed to be in sole possession of all-embracing truth considered absolute at any given moment, but liable to be superseded at any time by other, entirely different absolute truths as the result of some sudden fluctuation in the official line. Russia's rulers also believe, or profess to believe, that their creed and system of rule are destined to obtain eventual ascendancy over the entire globe as part of a historically determined process which loyal communists must promote by all means, fair or foul, but which is in any case bound to triumph in the end.

Claiming to rule with a special mandate from the working class, the totalitarian state prescribes a comprehensive set of obligatory views in virtually all spheres of thought, political and non-political. It demands the citizen's total allegiance, compelling affirmations and postures of assent by an elaborate system of rewards, and by penalties which have ranged from intensive exhortation to summary execution.

Within Soviet historiography thought control is applied with great severity. It is especially stringent in its impact on the history of Russia, as opposed to that of other lands, and becomes ever more rigorous as the historian's subject-matter approaches the present day. Much Russian history – especially the most modern – is, accordingly, a state secret, one closely but by no means effectively guarded. The Moscow-controlled historian is also required to stress the element of class struggle to a greater extent than would be accepted by most non-Marxists. Certain vague but key concepts – for example, 'feudal' and 'bourgeois' – are lavishly used in a function liturgical rather than descriptive. Another feature is extreme nationalism, Russian defeats being played down, and successful Russian initiatives evocatively commemorated, to a degree not always warranted by evidence.

Though deliberate mis-statements have not been a general characteristic of Moscow-controlled historiography, with the important exception of the Stalin period, the purposeful omission of inconvenient information remains a staple feature, as also is the careful loading of emphasis. Among intentional exclusions, the conversion into a virtual 'unperson' of the great revolutionary Leo Trotsky – one of the main architects of Bolshevik victory in the *coup d'état* of October 1917, as also in the Civil War of 1918–21 – remains outstanding, for this is as if twentieth-century British history were to be rewritten so as to exclude such a figure as Lloyd George. Yet even these gross defects of approach are far indeed from invalidating the work of Kremlin-instructed Russian historians as a whole, since the best of them are adept at making the prescribed gestures of conformity without great detriment to the body of their work. It is essential though, for non-Marxist students to approach their writings warily and with considerable knowledge of the compulsory postures, as also of the periodical changes in those postures, which are decreed from above.

Whether Kremlin-instructed or independently based, no student of the subject can fail to be struck by the exceptionally calamitous nature of Russian history since 1914. After bearing more than her proportional share of casualties in the First World War, Russia – unlike other major belligerents – was immediately plunged into three years of savage civil conflict which ushered in a great famine. A short period of comparative relaxation was then followed by two colossal bouts of self-destruction. In 1929–33 Stalin's collectivization of agriculture, culminating in a second great famine, destroyed unknown millions of peasants. No less devastating was Stalin's Great Terror, which reached its peak in 1937–38, and embraced the population as a whole. This led into the Second World War, the Russo-German campaign being fought largely on Soviet soil: possibly the most destructive episode in the entire history of warfare. Russian victory over the Germans then ushered in a period of increased domestic terror which was mild only by comparison with the worst years preceding the war, but was considerably reduced in scale after Stalin's death in 1953.

In modern times no other major industrial state, and certainly no English-speaking country, has yet suffered a chain of calamities remotely comparable. Earlier Russian history does, however, provide parallels, as will be shown below, in the Mongol-Tatar Yoke, the middle of Ivan the Terrible's reign, the Time of Troubles and the Napoleonic invasion of 1812. In tracing the history of Russia from earliest times, one is, accordingly, embarking on a tragic story in which heroism, injustice, courage, folly, stubborn resilience and sheer bad luck have all played their part. Moreover, tragedy – as will also be illustrated below – is often found mingled with more than a seasoning of grotesque comedy. The combination calls to mind the literary cliché coined to describe the atmosphere sometimes evoked by Gogol and other great nineteenth-century Russian writers: 'laughter through tears'.

Chapter Two

KIEV

The dawn of Russian history broke in the ninth century AD, when Kiev became the centre of a flourishing Old Russian community around the middle and upper reaches of the River Dnieper, in an area now forming part of the extreme western territory of the USSR. It was here, on an axis running between the cities of Novgorod and Kiev, and in a lozenge of land some eight hundred miles in length from north to south, being roughly half as wide, that eastern Slav tribes first began to form the rudiments of a state. Illiterate (for they as yet possessed no alphabet) and practising a primitive pagan religion, they were united chiefly by customs and language. Old Russian is the earliest extant eastern variety of the Slavonic language group, itself a member of the Indo-European family to which the majority of European tongues, including English, belong. Though the common Slavonic language has not survived, its western offshoot is chiefly represented by Polish, Czech and Slovak, and its southern variety by Serbo-Croat, Slovene and Bulgarian.

Old Russian survives in a variety of early manuscripts. Though a single language in earliest historical times, it has since split into three modern tongues: Russian, Ukrainian and Belorussian. As this reminds one, the original eastern Slavs, known to historians as Old Russians, were not the ancestors of the modern Russians alone, but also of the modern Ukrainians and Belorussians, for significant differences among the three peoples did not emerge until the thirteenth century. This helps to explain how Kiev, the capital of Old Russia, can now be the chief centre of the Ukraine, lying right outside the territory of the RSFSR – that is, of Russia proper. It also helps to explain why Old Russia included territory corresponding to lands now belonging to the Ukrainian and Belorussian, as well as to the Russian, constituent republics of the USSR. All three republics are thus the ultimate heirs of the medieval 'Rus': the term used by the Old Russians to describe both themselves and their lands. A word of much disputed origin, Rus is used in the present study as a rough synonym for the Old

Handle of a gold comb, showing
Scythian warriors in battle. Fourth
century BC.

Vase from Kul Oba, near Kerch,
showing a Scythian stringing a bow.
Fourth to third century BC.

Russian people generally, as also for their territories, in the historical period of eastern Slav unity.

Long before any Rus state emerged, the prairies of what is now southern European Russia had been ruled by a succession of peoples, mostly coming from the east. During the age of the Scythians, from the seventh century BC onwards, numerous Greek colonies were established on the shores of the Black Sea. The Scythians were followed by the Sarmatians (like their predecessors, an Iranian people), who held sway from the third century BC, during which time the Roman Empire absorbed the Greek colonies of the Black Sea Coast. In the third and fourth centuries AD southern Russia was dominated by Goths, who arrived from the north-west. They were followed by other intruders from the orient: Huns, Avars and Khazars. Nor did armed invasion from the east cease with the establishment of the first rudimentary Rus state. Two Turkic tribes in particular repeatedly harried the emerging community. First there were the Pechenegs, who ambushed and slew the Rus prince Svyatoslav by the Dnieper Rapids in 972, but were decisively defeated by his grandson Yaroslav the Wise in 1036. They were succeeded by the Polovtsians, who remained the chief enemy of Old Russia until both were overwhelmed in the last and mightiest of all avalanches from the east: the Mongol-Tatar invasion of 1237–40.

According to official doctrine, as accepted in the Imperial Russian period, a precise year, AD 862, marked the establishment of the Old Russian state, and the millennial anniversary of Russia was therefore duly celebrated in 1862. The year 862 was that in which – according to the first Russian Chronicle, compiled in the early twelfth century – the people of Novgorod called in Varangians (Vikings originating in Scandinavia) to rule over them and bring order into their affairs. The Varangian prince Ryurik became celebrated as the original founder of the main Russian princely line, that of the Ryurikids. Another Varangian prince, Oleg, established his capital at Kiev, becoming the first independent ruler of Kievan Rus in 882.

The role of the Varangians in founding the first Rus state remains controversial. On the one hand the first princes of Kiev bore Scandinavian names, as did many of their leading retainers, until the accession of Svyatoslav (the first Slavonic-named prince) in about 945. Half pirates, half merchantmen, the Varangians were prominent in exploiting the north–south trade route 'from the Varangians to the Greeks' – that is, from the Baltic, down Russian rivers and portages, through Kiev and the lower Dnieper, to the Black Sea and Constantinople. These merchant adventurers traded with and raided Constantinople,

Silver cover of a sabre sheath (eleventh to twelfth century AD) of the late Alanic kingdom in the northern Caucasus. The Alans were an Iranian-speaking people of Sarmatian origin.

13

St Vladimir, Grand Prince of Kiev
(reigned *c.* 980–1015). Seventeenth-
century book illustration.

Norse names being prominent in certain surviving tenth-century commercial treaties signed between Old Russia and the Byzantine Empire. The Varangians may also have been responsible for the name Rus, since it was probably they, rather than the native Slav population, who first bore this name. Be that as it may, the Varangians quickly adopted the Old Russian language and customs. They left little cultural trace on Rus history, only half a dozen borrowed Norse words having been traced in Old Russian. Nor have attempts to investigate Varangian influence on Old Russian law and religion led to impressive results. If the 'Norman theory' (that the first Russian state was essentially a Varangian creation) still retains any vitality, this is partly due to the fact that it has been out-lawed by Soviet historiography. All too often the Russians have been seen, and have seen themselves, as an inert, easy-going, lackadaisical people, incapable of political or other initiative, and requiring stimulus from outside, whether from a Georgian dictator such as Stalin or from their nineteenth-century emperors, who were overwhelmingly of Teutonic descent. The idea that the primitive Slavonic state could only have been galvanized into being by virile intruders from outside – and by the Germanic Varangians at that – has naturally proved unpalatable to Russian national pride.

The most important event in the emergence of early Russia was the adoption of Christianity as the official state religion with the conversion of the Kievan prince Vladimir in about 988. Later canonized, Vladimir was not in every way a saintly figure, for he was reputed to maintain a harem of eight hundred concubines, and is even described by a German chronicler of the period as *fornicator immensus et crudelis*. But whatever the character of his private life, the saint took an important step towards making Kievan Rus part of the general European community when he adopted Christianity. He also exposed Kiev to increased Byzantine cultural influence which became especially potent in painting and architecture. Both founded in eleventh-century Kiev, the Monastery of the Caves and St Sophia's Cathedral vied with each other as the two outstanding monuments of early Rus Christianity. The monastery was also notable as the home of the monks who first chronicled Old Russian history.

Conversion to Christianity was above all important in bringing literacy to the Rus, owing to the practice of using sacred texts couched in Old Church Slavonic: a language sufficiently close to the Old Russian vernacular to be immediately intelligible in Kiev. The modern Cyrillic alphabet of thirty-two letters owes its name to St Cyril, who, with his brother St Methodius, had been the first to translate biblical texts into a Slavonic dialect in about 863, while conducting a mission to the Slavs of Moravia.

Constantine IX Monomakh, Byzantine Emperor (reigned 1042–55), receives envoys from Kiev. The same envoys return to Kiev (*right*). From a thirteenth- or fourteenth-century Greek manuscript.

Four daughters of Yaroslav the Wise (reigned 1019–54). From a fresco in St Sophia's Cathedral, Kiev (*c.* 1045).

Right: Sarcophagus of Yaroslav the Wise. St Sophia's Cathedral, Kiev.

Particular importance attaches to St Vladimir's choice of the Eastern, or Orthodox, branch of Christianity as the official Russian state religion. Though the schism between Rome and Byzantium was not formalized until later (1054), the saintly fornicator's preference for Eastern Christianity was to have a lasting effect on Russian development, limiting the extent to which the Russians – as opposed to the Poles and Czechs, for example – could become an integral part of the European cultural community.

St Vladimir's son, Yaroslav the Wise, was an outstanding europeanizer, not least in his genealogical involvements. Three of his daughters became queens of western European states (France, Norway and Hungary). Of his sons, three married German princesses and another a Byzantine princess, he himself being a son-in-law of the King of Sweden and brother-in-law to the King of Poland. For equally intricate Russian dynastic involvements with western Europe, one has to wait for the nineteenth-century Romanov emperors.

The eight decades spanned by Vladimir's and Yaroslav's reigns (*c.* 980–1054) mark the peak of Kievan Russia's development. Yet it was during these years of prosperity that Kiev was plagued with attacks on her southern frontiers by Pechenegs and Polovtsians, the nomad Turkic tribes coming from the east. Nor was this period free from civil war, for the endemic curse of Russian history was already much in evidence: an inability to settle the succession to supreme power without strife. The death of Svyatoslav in 972 was followed, as that of

Vladimir in 1015 and that of Yaroslav in 1054, by civil war as various princely competitors sought to make good their claims to the throne of Kiev. Nor were matters improved after Yaroslav's death, when a rota system came into operation, the various principalities being graded in order of importance and the princes all moving up one step on the death of a senior ruler. Thus, in theory at least, the death of the Grand Prince of Kiev was to be followed by a general shift among all junior princes. In fact, force and guile came to exert increasing influence on the decisions. Nor has Russia yet been freed from this nuisance. Disputes over the succession were particularly common in the eighteenth century. The first and only Russian ruler to fashion an effective law of succession, Paul I (1796–1801), was himself assassinated a few years later, while succession struggles have, notoriously, not decreased in the Soviet period.

As already indicated, it was partly as a trading organization that the Old Russian state came into being. The Dnieper, the Volga and the Western Dvina, together with their manifold tributaries and the portages which linked them, served as the channels whereby forest products, notably fur, wax and honey, were ferried to Constantinople, there to be traded for cargoes of wine, silks, jewellery and other luxury goods. The Rus also maintained a lively commerce in human freight during this period when capture in battle, whether of fellow-Slavs or foreigners, normally led to the enslavement of prisoners, who might be ransomed, retained to serve Kievan masters, or exported for profit.

Despite the emphasis laid on trade by written historical sources, the Kievan economy now appears, from archaeological and other evidence, to have been basically agricultural, the land being tilled by various categories of peasants too humble to have captured the imagination of monkish chroniclers. Of the lowly status of agriculture the general name for a free peasant in the period – *smerd* ('stinker') – provides an eloquent indication. But important as agriculture was, Kievan Russia was also an urban civilization. There is evidence that it contained well over two hundred towns in its heyday, though some of these resembled stockaded trading-posts more than cities. The historian Vernadsky has reckoned the total population of twelfth-century Kievan Rus at seven to eight million, providing little evidence for so high a calculation. But in any case the country was one of the largest and most flourishing states in Europe at the time of its greatest prosperity.

Though Kievan Rus was a slave-owning and slave-trading society, it was also remarkably liberal in its political and social organization. The oldest sur-viving law code, *Russkaya pravda*, does not even make any provision for a death

Reconstruction of an eleventh-century Kievan peasant hut.

St Olga (*c.* 879–969), who acted as regent to her son Svyatoslav and was the grandmother of St Vladimir. An early Kievan convert to Christianity, she is shown here receiving instruction at the Byzantine court. Byzantine illuminated manuscript, thirteenth to fourteenth century.

penalty, while Kievan women enjoyed considerable status – one of them, the redoubtable Princess Olga, acting as regent during the minority of her son Svyatoslav. Nor does the Kievan state appear to have contained seeds of autocracy such as were later to sprout so vigorously on the soil of Muscovy. Even during the brief periods when the whole realm was effectively ruled by a single supreme prince (Vladimir and Yaroslav), it resembled a loose federation of princedoms rather than an absolute monarchy. The notables – members of the prince's bodyguard and others, who came to be called boyars – were, at this stage of Russian history, free to transfer their allegiance from one ruler to another. There also existed, in Kiev and in the capitals of the various princedoms, a traditional democratic institution: the *veche*. This was less a parliament than a gathering of all adult free male citizens, and has been compared to the assembly of ancient Athens. Its powers varied from period to period and from city to city, but there were occasions when it could appoint or dismiss a ruling prince, and decide whether or not to go to war.

Yaroslav the Wise was the last prince to rule over Kievan Rus as a whole. After his death in 1054 the territory dissolved into a dozen component princedoms, of which Kiev itself was only one. Under Prince Vladimir Monomakh, who ruled in Kiev from 1113 to 1125, the country was briefly reunited, at least to the extent that some three-quarters of it came under Monomakh's control in accordance with his policy of combining the Russian principalities in common defence against the Polovtsian enemy. Yet his reign provided but a short respite from gradual disintegration. Nomad raiders now drove the Russians off the lower Dnieper, thus hampering trade with Constantinople – traffic which was also impeded by Venetian success in capturing commercial routes through the Mediterranean. Thus Kiev fell into commercial and political decline.

Meanwhile three other principalities on the periphery came into prominence.

In the south-west, Galicia and Volhynia were temporarily united under Prince Roman and became remarkable for the degree of influence wielded by the aristocratic element as embodied in the Council of Boyars.

In the north a special role was played by Novgorod, which had developed into a great colonizing power, extending its sway over sparsely inhabited territory greater in area than that of the rest of Rus put together. Novgorod was also remarkable for the development of democratic institutions. The *veche*, the popular assembly of townsfolk, exercised considerable influence, and the Novgorodians took to electing their own princes as military leaders, being careful to limit their power and even forbidding them to own land within Novgorodian territory. Considerable political power was also exercised by Novgorod's archbishops and mayors. All in all, Novgorod came as near to realizing the concept of the city-state as any other Old Russian town.

The most significant development of the period, though it barely seemed so at the time, was that of Vladimir-Suzdal (Novgorod's eastern neighbour-principality) as the cradle of Great Russia. Situated in forest land lying away from the steppes and sparsely inhabited by Finnic tribes, the area began to attract immigrants from the declining lands around Kiev. In the forests of the north-east these were able to find refuge from the raids of prairie nomads. Another important feature of Vladimir-Suzdal was a tendency for the monarchic principle to predominate over the democratic and aristocratic, as favoured in

The walls of the Novgorod Kremlin, built during the fourteenth and fifteenth centuries.

Prince Andrew Bogolyubsky goes to war. Detail from
a painting in the Church of the Virgin, Novgorod.
Right: The Uspensky Cathedral, Vladimir, built 1158–61.

Novgorod and Galicia-Volhynia respectively. One north-eastern prince in
particular, Andrew Bogolyubsky, has appealed to the imagination of historians
as a man born before his time – a would-be autocrat who sought to realize the
later ambitions of Ivan the Great, Ivan the Terrible and others by bringing all
the Rus lands under his sway. In 1169 his armies captured and sacked Kiev. It
was a symptom of Kiev's decline that Prince Andrew did not choose to set up
his own capital there, as he might have done, but returned to hold power in
Vladimir, where he built the Uspensky Cathedral and other churches and
monasteries. Brought into conflict with his leading boyars by his authoritarian
tendencies, Andrew Bogolyubsky was assassinated in 1174, once again foreshadowing the future course of Russian history, in which the murder of Tsars
and Emperors was to become a common occurrence.

Vladimir was already the third capital (after Rostov and Suzdal) of Vladimir-
Suzdal at a time when no twelfth-century Russian could suspect that the
principality would eventually acquire its fourth and final capital in Moscow.
Only a small provincial centre at this time, Moscow is first mentioned in the
Russian Chronicles under the date 1147. It was to owe its eventual dominant
position to an ability to grow and extend its influence under the conditions of
Tatar domination.

The Tatars and the Rise of Moscow

After more than three hundred years of independence the Rus lands were conquered and devastated by invading oriental hordes in 1237–40, thus embarking on a period of more than two centuries' foreign domination. This calamity is known as the Tatar Yoke.

The invaders whom the Russians called Tatars belonged to the gigantic and recently expanded Mongol Empire of Jenghiz Khan, who had died in 1227. They consisted of Turkic peoples under a small Mongol ruling élite which itself adopted Turkic speech in due course. It is easier to say when the Yoke began than when it ended, since the Tatars gradually weakened and retreated after an initial period of about a hundred years during which their overlordship bore most severely and extensively on the Rus. From the early fourteenth century onwards, large areas of western Rus – including all modern Belorussia and a large area of the modern Ukraine – were progressively relieved of Tatar domination, becoming part of the fast-expanding state of Lithuania. What had formerly belonged to the western fringe of the Mongol Empire was thus gradually exchanging a harsh eastern for a relatively mild western master.

A period which ended with the invaders' gradual expulsion and retreat had begun with a sudden explosion of fury in December 1237 when the Mongol Khan Baty, grandson of Jenghiz Khan, hurled his cavalry across the Volga and attacked Ryazan, the first Russian town to be assaulted. Falling after a five-day siege, Ryazan was sacked and destroyed. Then Moscow – fortified, but still only a small town – was captured and burnt to the ground. Vladimir's turn followed. By this winter onslaught on north-eastern Russia, the Tatars proved themselves a foe terrible and powerful beyond any in previous Russian history. It was their custom, on seizing a city, to massacre all or most of the inhabitants, enslaving those whom they did not choose to kill, while looting or burning all property. It is hardly surprising that the Rus, in this age of general piety, saw the Tatars as a scourge sent by God to punish them for their sins.

After the first storming attack, the Tatars stopped short of Novgorod, their movements over the no longer frozen rivers and terrain hampered by the thaw of spring 1238. They turned south to regroup before mounting another great offensive in 1240, when they utterly destroyed Kiev, Chernigov, Pereyaslav and other towns of southern Russia. Baty's campaigns also took him into Europe, as far as Hungary, and he was deterred from conquests yet further west only when news arrived of the death in Mongolia of his suzerain, the Great Khan Ugedey. The conqueror now turned his armies back from Europe in order to claim the

◀ Battle between Novgorod and Suzdal. Fifteenth-century painting.

Jenghiz Khan.

succession. Disappointed of the great khanship, but retaining control over the vast western province which included Rus among its extreme outposts, Baty set up his capital at Saray on the lower Volga, and ruled as a vassal of his successful rival, the newly appointed Great Khan. The realm of Baty and his successors later acquired the name Golden Horde.

On the extent of Tatar devastation much evidence survives in the Russian Chronicles, in the Russian Lives of Saints and in other literature from this age of general lamentation. One of the rare visitors to Russia from the west has also left vivid testimony on conditions in the former capital city. This was the papal envoy John of Plano Carpini, who travelled through southern Russia in 1246 on his way to Mongolia. He reported that the Tatars had killed the inhabitants of Kiev after besieging it in 1240. In what had been one of the greatest cities of medieval Europe, they had left barely two hundred houses standing, countless skulls and bones were scattered over the whole countryside, and the few survivors had been enslaved. After a long period of decline, Kiev thus passes temporarily out of Russian history, though remaining the nominal centre of the Russian Orthodox Church until the fifteenth century.

The Golden Horde was a destructive and predatory organization geared to exploit Russians as a source of slaves, army recruits and tribute, often in the form of furs and other forest produce. In general, these contributions were not exacted through military occupation or by direct rule. Finding Russia divided into separate principalities, the Tatars left some local Russian princes and princelings to preside semi-impotently over their ruined dominions, making them responsible, after a brief period under Tatar collectors, for gathering tribute by a system resembling the protection racket as operated by criminal organizations in modern times. Contributions were assessed through periodical censuses carried out by the Tatars, who also conscripted Russians into their armies on the basis of one out of every ten males. Surviving census data have made it possible to assess the overall Rus population during the Tatar period – but very tentatively – at about ten million souls.

Failure to meet Tatar requisitions brought down drastic reprisals in the form of further massacre, looting and enslavement through punitive expeditions carried out by garrisons poised to terrorize the recalcitrant. Russian princes were generally allowed to succeed to their various thrones in accordance with the cumbrous and inconvenient traditions which they had inherited from Kievan times, but newly succeeding princes had to obtain a patent from the Tatar authorities by journeying to Mongol headquarters. By recognizing the rulers of certain areas as grand princes with delegated authority over lesser princelings, the Tatars reduced the problems of administration.

Kaunas Castle in Lithuania. In 1362 it was destroyed by the Teutonic Knights.

St Alexander Nevsky (*c.* 1220–63).
Detail from a mural in the Arkhangelsky
Cathedral, Moscow.

The Tatars embraced Islam in the fourteenth century, but were outstandingly tolerant in their treatment of the Russian Church. Far from persecuting Orthodoxy, they exempted the clergy and monasteries from taxation. The Church's privileged position under the Tatars enhanced its status as a spiritual haven and unifying factor in an age of terror and suffering. It was an index of the Church's growing prestige that one metropolitan, St Alexis, acted as *de facto* head of government under two successive Grand Princes of Moscow.

Though the régime established by the Tatars encompassed almost the entire territory of Rus during the first century of the Yoke, a small area in the north-west remained immune from conquest and the levy of tribute. Nor did the Tatars actually conquer the far-flung principality of Novgorod, for the Prince of Novgorod chose to submit and pay voluntary tribute in view of overwhelming Tatar military strength. Yet the prince in question, Alexander Nevsky, also became renowned as a great war hero, and at the very time of the Tatar onslaught – against different enemies coming from the opposite direction. He decisively defeated the Swedes on the Neva in 1240 (hence the title Nevsky added to his name), and then routed the Livonian knights on the ice of Lake Peipus in 1242. As a vassal of the Golden Horde, Alexander paid several visits to the Mongol court at Saray, where he deployed diplomatic skills to ease the impact of Tatar dominion on his subjects as Prince of Novgorod and later as Grand Prince of Vladimir. Such services helped to recommend him for canonization, and his remains were later removed to the St Alexander Nevsky Monastery in St Petersburg by Peter the Great. In 1942 the saint's posthumous fate received an unexpected twist through the institution of a Soviet decoration, the Order of Alexander Nevsky, in his honour.

Alexander's son, Daniel, became Prince of Moscow, thus founding the Muscovite dynasty which came to rule the expanding principality for over three centuries, from 1276 through an unbroken line of twelve princes or grand princes and ten generations until the death of Theodore I in 1598. As this reminds one, the outstanding Russian development of the period was the rise of Moscow, under the cloak of foreign overlordship, from an insignificant minor principality to the point where it eventually emerged from the Tatar Yoke as the capital city of the first centralized independent Russian state.

Territorially speaking, Moscow's expansion took place in several gulps. The first swift and comparatively minor gains occurred under Prince Daniel at the beginning of the fourteenth century. Ruling an area tiny by Russian standards (about 120 miles wide from west to east, and about 70 deep), he more than doubled his holdings by annexing lands in the south, north-east and west. A long lull followed, Moscow's ascendancy being consolidated – but without formal annexation of territory – under Ivan I Kalita ('Moneybag'). It was during the reigns of Dmitry Donskoy (1359–89) and Vasily I (1389–1425) that Muscovite territorial gains under the Tatars were most impressive, the principality expanding about eightfold within some seven decades. This series of giant gulps was again followed by a comparative lull in the reign of Vasily II (1425–62). But that setback was merely a prelude to the further large expansion of Muscovy under Ivan III (the Great), to be considered below.

Moscow's expansion was far more than a mere territorial process, being also accompanied by a vast increase in prestige. Advancing from a small principality to a grand principality with its own subject princes, and swallowing up the former Grand Principality of Vladimir, Moscow also became the residence and *de facto* seat of the Metropolitanate of the Russian Church, from 1326 onwards. Both the Metropolitan resident in Moscow and the Muscovite Grand Prince began to include in their official titles the significant *vseya Rusi* ('of All Rus') – the phrase so commonly and perversely mis-translated as 'of All the Russias'.

Historians have much canvassed the reasons for Moscow's rise to supremacy over the many competing Russian principalities, the following factors being prominent among those cited. Lying between the Volga and the Oka at a

Star of the Order of Alexander Nevsky, the Soviet decoration instituted in 1942.

27

A Moscow Grand Prince
in his Kremlin.

particularly strategic point on the great river network which provided access to all parts of the European Russian plain, Moscow was favourably placed to trade and move troops. Somewhat at variance with this is another claim commonly advanced: that Moscow rose to pre-eminence through its very inaccessibility. Surrounded by uninhabited forests, the city was (according to this theory) less exposed to attack than other centres, consequently attracting more settlers from outside and acquiring a swiftly expanding population. Other comparatively accidental factors may also be mentioned. Moscow's princes happened to be particularly long-lived, the average duration of their reigns being more than a quarter of a century per sovereign. They also tended to have few sons, so that the always thorny problem of succession to the throne was minimized. Not generally regarded as great military leaders, Muscovite rulers were credited with unusual guile in ingratiating themselves with the Tatars, in pursuing material gain and in discreetly deserting their armies on the eve of battle.

No doubt all these considerations were important, but perhaps the overriding cause of Muscovite success lay in the Tatars' desire to preserve a balance of power in Russia as a whole. Holding the Rus in an iron grip, yet by remote control, succeeding Khans followed the policy of playing off one principality against another. In the early fourteenth century, Saray encouraged Moscow as a

The Battle of Kulikovo, 1380. A sixteenth-century manuscript illustration.

rival to the arguably more powerful Grand Principality of Tver. The eclipse of Tver was followed in the mid-fourteenth century by the further expansion of Lithuania – a state not subject to Saray and itself a growing threat to the Tatars. Moscow was, accordingly, now valued by the Tatars as a centre of resistance to Lithuanian encroachments. According to this theory, Moscow may have benefited from its very weakness, since this earned favourable treatment by the Tatars which permitted Muscovite expansion as a counterweight to more powerful competitors.

In favouring Moscow, the Tatars had to be careful not to allow their protégé to become dangerous to themselves. They received a sharp lesson to this effect in 1380 when a rebel Russian army under Prince Dmitry of Moscow defeated the Tatar potentate Mamay at Kulikovo Field near the River Don, whence the Prince received the title Donskoy ('of the Don'). The victory greatly stimulated Russian morale, but without becoming a decisive turning-point in the overthrow of the Tatar Yoke, for the Tatars returned in force under Khan Tokhtamysh two years later. Though Moscow was now defended by artillery, this being the first occasion on which the possession of cannon by Russians is recorded in the Chronicles, Tokhtamysh seized the city by trickery, devastated it and laid Muscovy under tribute again.

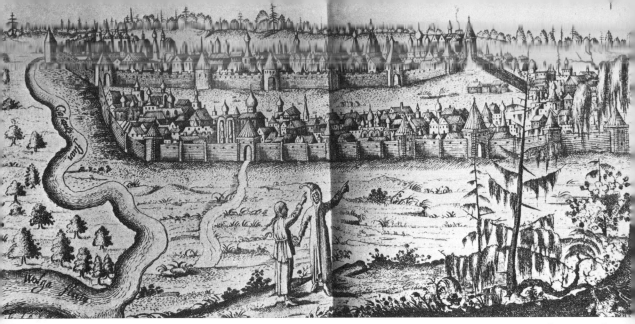

Kazan, formerly capital of the Tatar Khanate on the River Volga. Engraving by O. Koch.

The gradual ending of the Yoke owed more to internal Tatar disputes than to Russian military exertions. In the early fifteenth century, Tatar dissensions caused separate khanates – those of Kazan, the Crimea and Astrakhan – to split away from the Golden Horde.

The impact of the Tatar Yoke on Russia has been much discussed, and though individual interpretations vary greatly, the episode is generally agreed to have been disastrous. The Tatars slaughtered untold thousands of Russians, inflicting serious damage on the economy – and especially on the towns – by the practice of looting, burning and kidnapping on so vast a scale. As a matter of deliberate policy they robbed Russia of skilled craftsmen, deporting them to Tatary in quantity. The Tatars also retarded Russia's advance as a member of the European community by erecting a formidable prototype of the later Iron Curtain. During the Tatar period, Russian princes were not permitted to conduct foreign policy, and practically all contact with western Europe was suspended – hence, possibly, the absence in Russian development of anything resembling the Renaissance and Reformation. Hence too the claim, commonly made, that the Tatars retarded Russia's progress by several centuries. Above all the Tatar Khans – or Tsars, as the Russians began to call them – provided a model of extreme authoritarian rule combined with control through terror such as could be countered only by submissiveness, duplicity and quick-witted readiness to betray one's fellow-princes before they betrayed oneself. These were heavy penalties to pay in exchange for a rudimentary postal system, a handful of Turkic loan-words, the practice of keeping Russian women in seclusion, and the custom of banging one's forehead on the ground to signify respect for a superior.

As noted above, the Tatars gradually yielded western Rus to the Lithuanian Princedom. By the early fifteenth century this state had greatly expanded, even reaching the Black Sea coast under Grand Prince Vitovt (ruled 1392–1430). The Lithuanians themselves formed only a small minority in a country governed on federal principles allowing considerable regional autonomy. Lithuanian rule was, accordingly, milder than Tatar domination. Nor could the Rus of the Tatar period, whether inside or outside Lithuania, regard that state as wholly foreign, especially as the official language was medieval Belorussian. But there was also an alienating factor in the close association of Lithuania with Poland signalized by the signing of the Union of Krevo between the two countries (1385) and the consequent adoption by Lithuania of Catholicism as her official state religion. This began the process, eventually completed through the Union of Lublin (1569), whereby Lithuania and Poland became a single state.

Separate development under Lithuanian-Polish rule was the main factor leading to the break-up of the eastern Slavs into the three branches of the present day: the Ukrainians and Belorussians on the one hand (Tatar-dominated for about one century) and the Russians proper, also known as the Great Russians (Tatar-dominated for over two hundred years).

EARLY MUSCOVY

Succeeding to the Grand Princedom of Moscow at the age of twenty-two, Ivan III ruled from 1462 to 1505, his tenure of power as an adult being longer than that of any other Russian sovereign or dictator. So impressive were his achievements that historians have sometimes called him the Great: a title which he shares with Peter I and Catherine II among other Russian rulers, Peter being the only one of the three on whom the honorific was conferred by official decree. Himself a collector of impressive titles, Ivan III would certainly have appreciated having greatness thrust upon him by historians, but though he was probably the most effective of all Muscovy's rulers, he perhaps fell short of true grandeur in that his horizons were unduly bounded by the mechanics of power-seeking and power-keeping. To these processes he brought high technical expertise, being superbly attuned to the military and administrative possibilities of his day. Reputedly so awesome in appearance that women trembled and fainted at the mere sight of him, he was yet no outstanding military hero, preferring whenever possible to win his victories away from the battlefield, by guile and patience. Such was the chief unifier of the Great Russian people, the main architect of early Muscovite absolutism and the liberator of his subjects from the last remnants of thraldom to Tatary.

Tatar overlordship finally petered out in 1480 when Akhmed, Khan of the Great Horde (successor-state to the truncated Golden Horde), led an army against Moscow to exact tribute withheld during the previous four years by Grand Prince Ivan. The episode ended after Tatar and Muscovite armies had faced each other across the River Ugra, west of Ivan's capital, for several weeks without joining combat. Akhmed then decided to retreat, being disappointed of help promised by his temporary ally, the King of Poland, but was ambushed and killed on his way back to Saray by rival Tatar princelings – who were possibly acting on the suggestion of the Grand Prince of Moscow. As this possibility indicates, Ivan was now exploiting Tatar rivalries, just as the Tatars themselves had once been accustomed to play off one Russian prince against another. In particular, Ivan cultivated an alliance with Akhmed's enemy, Mengli-Girey, the Khan of the Crimean Tatars – who had, incidentally, come under the suzerainty of the Turkish Sultan in 1475.

Though Russia was no longer a dependency of the Tatars after 1480 – and the Great Horde was itself destroyed by Mengli-Girey in 1502 – murderous Tatar raids on Muscovy by no means ceased, and the Muscovites continued to maintain a defensive barrier against them on the line of the River Oka. Even after the conquest of the Kazan and Astrakhan Khanates by Ivan the Terrible in the middle of the sixteenth century, the Crimean Tatars still posed a threat. They continued to harass Russia until the annexation of the Crimea by Catherine the Great in the late eighteenth century, after which the Tatars became more familiar as waiters in Moscow restaurants than as the dreaded horsemen from the southern prairies.

It was over his fellow-countrymen, rather than over the Tatars or any other foreign enemy, that Ivan III's main victories were gained. So successful were his expansionist policies that he increased the area of his realm about fourfold from the 160,000-odd square miles which he had inherited at his succession. Resembling a clumsy letter G in mirror-writing, that awkwardly shaped patrimony had clearly required rounding off, but few could have predicted that the young ruler would consolidate so successfully as to advance many hundreds of miles in every direction except the south-east. Certain minor princedoms or estates came to him through purchase, intimidation or voluntary submission, while others were annexed by outright military conquest. The acquisitions included Yaroslavl, Rostov and Tver in the centre already half swallowed by the Muscovite boa-constrictor before Ivan's accession. There were also extensive gains in the south-west, including Chernigov. But the most important acquisition was Novgorod, together with its far-flung northern colonial territories which reached to the White Sea, the Arctic Ocean, and even beyond the northern Urals.

Ivan's subjugation of Novgorod was a gradual affair, and included two military campaigns in 1471 and 1478. A firm champion of absolutism, the Grand Prince was at pains to crush the vanquished city-state's political institutions, replacing its oligarchic and democratic practices with his own autocratic rule, and removing to Moscow the *veche* bell which had for so long summoned Novgorodian popular assemblies. Ivan also pioneered, or at least greatly developed, a custom which was to be followed by later rulers of Russia – including particularly Ivan the Terrible and Stalin – when he ordered the mass deportation of many thousand Novgorodian citizens. He dispatched them to the interior, settling politically reliable Muscovites on their original lands. Similar procedures were followed on a lesser scale in Tver, as also by Ivan's son and successor, Vasily III, when he further extended his father's gains by taking

Astrakhan at the mouth of the River Volga, showing the old Tatar town (top right).

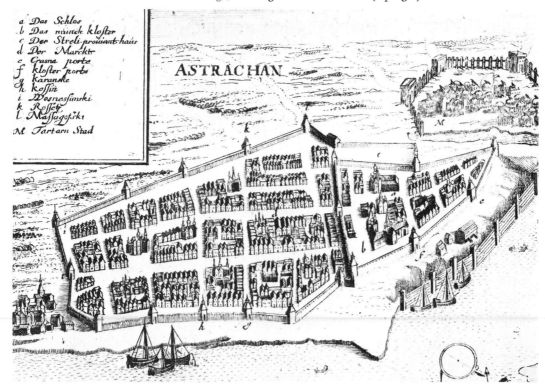

a Das Schlos
b Das münch kloster
c Der Streli-proiuant-haus
d Der Marckt
e Crasna porte
f kloster porte
g karanske
h kossir
i Wosnessinski
k Rossei
L Massagoszki
M Tartarn Stad

ASTRACHAN

33

Grand Prince Ivan III of Moscow
(Ivan the Great: reigned
1462–1505) and his family.
Detail from a tapestry of 1498.

Pskov and the remaining Ryazan lands. Grand Prince Vasily also annexed Smolensk, and thus completed the incorporation of virtually all the Great Russian people within Moscow's sway.

Though Ivan was also eager to bring the western Rus (the future Belorussia and Ukraine) under his control, the war which he fought against Lithuania to this end in 1500–03 proved indecisive. Here Ivan the Great was anticipating both the military failures of Ivan the Terrible and the final successes of Peter the Great in the Baltic area, while introducing a century and a half of intermittent warfare between Muscovy and Poland-Lithuania.

As a domestic administrator Ivan increased his personal power by a variety of means, evolving ingenious devices for bringing his subjects more closely

Peasants clearing the land. Illustration from the Radziwill Chronicle (fifteenth century).

under his control. In particular, he did much to destroy the old tradition, deriving from the Kievan period, whereby minor princelings had enjoyed the right to switch allegiance from one overlord to another at will. The effect of Ivan's conquests was to leave only one rival overlord in the field: the Grand Prince of Lithuania. Choosing to regard defection to Lithuania as treason, Ivan discouraged it by banishment, incarceration in monasteries, execution and the practice of requiring a suspect subject's associates to provide financial guarantees for his good conduct. Ivan's Law Code of 1497 was, incidentally, remarkable for the introduction of capital punishment – which, though previously inflicted, had not been legally countenanced within Muscovy. Another important technique of control was a change in the system of land tenure. Whereas land had once been held as the owner's full property, new grants became increasingly dependent on the performance of services. In other words, land was now awarded as a military fief, continued tenure being dependent on the holder's discharge of his duties to the sovereign.

An especially bizarre feature of the period was the growth of a system whereby civil and military appointments – as also matters of formal precedence – were determined on grounds of competing genealogical claims, the positions to which a given boyar or prince could aspire being determined by comparing them with appointments held by his forbears. This system fostered unsuitable promotions especially disastrous on the field of battle, but it proved extremely tenacious. It placed the Muscovite Grand Prince in the curious situation of being unable to allot seats at his own banqueting table among those on whom he could impose summary banishment or execution with comparative ease.

In keeping with his towering ambitions, Ivan was not satisfied to be a mere grand prince. Though he once rejected the offer of a kingly title (proffered by an envoy of the German Emperor) as beneath his dignity, he assumed the rank of Sovereign of All Rus: a deliberate challenge to the Grand Prince of Lithuania as ruler of the western Rus. He further assumed the title of 'autocrat', which at this time denoted the ruler of an independent state. Ivan also tentatively insisted on being addressed by the awesome title 'Tsar', hitherto confined to Tatar potentates, the Byzantine Emperor and various august biblical rulers. But not until 1547 was a Muscovite sovereign, Ivan III's grandson, formally crowned as Tsar.

Ivan sought further aggrandizement through wedlock. Widowed after marriage to a princess of Tver, he accepted as his second grand princess Sophia Paleologue, a niece of Constantine XI, the last Byzantine Emperor. In keeping with this choice of bride, Ivan also adopted the two-headed eagle of Byzantium as his emblem and replaced the homespun customs of the earlier Moscow court with imported pomp smacking of Byzantine practices. But there is little evidence that these innovations were the result of Sophia's direct influence, as is sometimes asserted. Nor is there evidence that she sought to convert her august consort to the Roman Catholic or Uniate faith, though it had been hoped by the Vatican that such a role might be played by the Rome-educated bride at the time when her betrothal to Grand Prince Ivan was under negotiation.

A typical Russian ruler in many ways, Ivan showed his national temper with especial vigour in his robust defence of the Orthodox faith, the practice of

Far left: The wedding of Ivan the Great and Sophia Paleologue. Miniature from the Litsevoy Chronicles of the late sixteenth century. *Left:* Manuscript illustration showing the celebrated ecclesiastical artist Andrew Rublyov (*c.* 1360–1430) as he paints a fresco in the Andronikov Monastery, Moscow.

A plan of Constantinople drawn in 1453 by Buondelmonte.

which was closely identified with Muscovite and pan-Russian patriotism. It was on a surge of combined national and religious enthusiasm that Muscovy first embraced full independence. Before Ivan's accession Metropolitan Isidore of Russia, himself of Greek nationality, had gravely offended his flock by accepting the union of the Eastern and Western Churches as negotiated at the Ferrara-Florence Conference of 1438–39, for which offence he incurred arrest on his return to Moscow. Isidore and the Union were repudiated, and ten years later a new Metropolitan, the Russian Jonas, was elevated independently of the Patriarch of Constantinople – who had hitherto appointed the heads of the Russian Church. This date therefore marks the emergence of the Russian Orthodox Church as an autocephalous organization: an episode so significant in the process of national self-assertion that its five hundredth anniversary was lavishly celebrated in officially atheist Soviet Russia in 1949. When Constantinople fell to the Turks in 1453, Russians regarded this catastrophe as divine retribution visited on the Eastern Church for accepting (temporarily) a union with Rome. In 1461 the Russians removed 'of Kiev' from their metropolitan's title, which henceforward read 'of Moscow and All Russia'. Now proudly conscious of its new status as the only independent Orthodox state, Muscovy began to see itself as the centre of Christendom, a doctrine promulgated by the monk Philotheus in a celebrated letter of 1510 to Grand Prince Vasily III. Rome and Constantinople having both fallen, their place (Philotheus asserted) was to be taken by Moscow as the Third Rome, which would last for all time, never giving way to a fourth.

Russian envoys arriving at the court of
Maximilian I, 1516. Eighteenth-century
woodcut.

Right: The Moscow Kremlin. Part of the
walls, showing the bell tower of
Ivan the Great.

Various dissensions troubled the Russian Church of this period. There was
the heresy of the Judaizers which arose in Novgorod, and there was the rift over
whether monasteries should hold property or not. But neither heresies nor
controversies prevented the Church from acting in close concert with the
Grand Prince, or from promulgating on Muscovite soil the Byzantine doctrine
of caesaropapism. The supreme ruler and the Church each gained enhanced
prestige from the expression of mutual admiration and esteem, while the Grand
Prince was all along clearly the senior partner. It was he, in the last resort, who
determined or confirmed appointments to the crucial office of Metropolitan.

Ivan the Great's reign was not least remarkable for the establishment of
contacts with western Europe such as had been severely restricted under the
Tatars. Foreign architects, builders and physicians, together with goldsmiths
and other craftsmen, came to Moscow – and despite the risks to which this
might expose them, for they were far from enjoying diplomatic immunity.
Official embassies were also exchanged, since Moscow now took up formal
relations with the Turkish Sultan, the Vatican, the Holy Roman Empire and
other foreign courts. Muscovite envoys were noted for being very much on their
dignity, and for their habit of withdrawing from official functions if they
considered themselves treated with inadequate ceremony.

Further symptoms of Moscow's rampant self-esteem included an elaborately mendacious official ideology whereby, for example, the Grand Princes of Moscow were described as ultimately descended from one Prus, a brother of the Roman Emperor Augustus and the reputed ancestor of the Prussians – and hence, by a further leap of fantasy, of the Russians. Another tradition of the period attributed a spurious provenance to the grand-princely crown and vestments: allegedly bestowed on the Kievan Prince Vladimir Monomakh by the Byzantine Emperor Constantine Monomakh. In keeping with this quest for grandeur, the Moscow Kremlin was very largely rebuilt during the reigns of Ivan the Great and his son. The huge brick walls and towers erected in 1485–95 survive almost unchanged to the present day. It was in this period, too, that several imposing cathedrals were constructed in the Kremlin precincts. They included the Uspensky Cathedral where all the Tsars, Emperors and Empresses of Russia were to be crowned, from the sixteenth to the nineteenth century, and also the Arkhangelsky Cathedral, where the Muscovite Grand Princes and Tsars are buried. This elaborate building programme owed much to the work of Italian architects.

Left: Ivan the Great. *Right:* Helen, Grand Princess of Moscow, and her infant son Ivan the Terrible as they supervise the minting of coinage. Miniature from a sixteenth-century Russian chronicle.

Thus the Muscovite Grand Prince and his court embarked on an epoch of self-glorification which becomes understandable when one remembers the prolonged humiliations inflicted on Russia by the Tatars. But though enhanced prestige and national self-confidence were exhilarating to many, they could seem an unmixed blessing only to those who favoured the concentration of absolute power in the person of the Muscovite sovereign. Of the giant strides already taken along this road, Baron von Herberstein – twice ambassador of the Holy Roman Empire to Moscow under Vasily III – provides eloquent testimony. Herberstein claims that Vasily's authority over his people was greater than that of any other monarch in the world. He 'holds unlimited control over all his subjects' lives and property. None of his counsellors has sufficient authority to dare oppose him, or even differ from him. . . . They openly proclaim that the Prince's will is God's will.'

IVAN THE TERRIBLE

In 1533 the Muscovite Grand Princedom passed to Ivan IV, a three-year-old boy and the elder son of Vasily III. Better known to a later age as Ivan the Terrible, the child eventually became the first in that sequence of especially potent, larger-than-life rulers of Russia who have fired the imagination of posterity throughout the ages. All these super-rulers – who also include Peter the Great, Catherine the Great, Lenin and Stalin – employed political terror in defence of their persons and governmental systems. But whereas the brutalities of a Peter, a Catherine, and even of a Lenin, were not wildly out of proportion to their political aims, Ivan the Terrible and Stalin practised extravagant overkill, slaughtering their subjects on a scale defying rational explanation.

Ivan's minority provided only sketchy hints of his terrible future. From the age of three until he was seven the infant despot lived under the regency of his mother, the Grand Princess Helen, who had become the second female ruler (after the tenth-century Princess Olga) of a country later to be dominated by its eighteenth-century empresses. Herself of western Russian origin, but also reputedly a descendant of the Tatar potentate Mamay, the Regent successfully quelled domestic feuds. She also repressed alien encroachment from Lithuania and Sweden, in which policies she was aided by a politically active lover, one of the many Princes Obolensky. In 1538, however, the Princess died, reputedly murdered by poison, after which a decade of chaos ensued.

Now, if ever, was a time when the aristocracy of princes and boyars could have asserted a claim to power and led a movement away from autocratic absolutism. But the Russian notables of 1538–47 were too busy quarrelling and plundering the leaderless grand princedom to unite in defence of their collective interests. One effect of this period of 'boyar rule' – for which 'boyar feuding' would be a better term – was to increase the impact of later despotism by inflaming in the temporarily helpless young Grand Prince Ivan acute lifelong resentments such as prompted him to wreak a bloody vengeance many years later. Slighting, neglecting, endangering or patronizing the juvenile sovereign in the 1540s, various titled hooligans helped to create in him the paranoiac mentality which eventually found its outlet in massacres sparing neither princes nor peasants.

By no means passive during his boyhood, Ivan was already arranging for the murder and ill-treatment of enemies real or fancied, but such early vicious tendencies were comparatively little in evidence in the early period of his active rule (1547–60). This was the time of his first marriage, to Anastasia Zakharyin

Tsar Ivan IV (Ivan the Terrible; reigned 1533–84) at the siege of Kazan, 1552. Detail from a sixteenth-century icon.

– an indirect forbear of the Romanov dynasty which was later to succeed to the Russian throne. Ivan married at the age of sixteen, being crowned in the same year, 1547, with lavish ceremony in Moscow's Uspensky Cathedral as 'Tsar of All Russia'. He thus became the first Muscovite sovereign to be crowned with this august title.

Ivan's greatest contribution to the growth of Muscovy came from military campaigns conducted against the Tatars of the east and south-east during the early years of his reign. Whereas Ivan III had slid out of the Tatar Yoke rather than overthrown it, shunning direct military conflict, his grandson now personally took the war into the enemy camp. In 1552 the Tsar stormed and captured Kazan after a six-week siege. Four years later he made himself master of Astrakhan. Each a Tatar khanate and each part-heir to the defunct Golden Horde, the two realms were absorbed by Muscovy, which now embraced the course of the Volga in its entirety. It was with this expansion, too, that Muscovy – ethnically unified by earlier rulers as the home of the Great Russians – first embarked on its remarkable career as nucleus of a multi-racial state, acquiring new citizens from a variety of non-Slavic peoples in addition to the Tatar: the Bashkirs, Cheremises, Chuvashes, Mordvinians and others. These gains were followed, in the last years of Ivan's reign, by the first significant Russian penetration of Asia. The Cossack leader Yermak invaded the Tatar Khanate of Siberia at the head of a few hundred troops and destroyed it, occupying the capital, Kashlyk, in 1582. Yermak himself was ambushed and killed by the ousted Khan Kuchum, but occupation of western Siberia continued apace with the foundation of numerous Russian settlements. Taken together, the gains under Ivan and his son Theodore I (who succeeded in 1584) more or less doubled Muscovite territory through the acquisition of a huge belt of land, varying in width between 150 and 600 miles, in the east and south-east.

During the early years of Ivan's reign important domestic reforms were enacted under the influence of two men of lowly origin whom the young Tsar chose as his closest counsellors. These were a priest, Sylvester, and a member of the minor gentry, Adashev. Their ascendancy saw the overhaul of the legal system with the publication of a new law code. Local government was also reformed through measures designed to protect provincials from the rapacity of administrators appointed by the centre. Then there were various ecclesiastical

Ivan the Terrible and his boyars after the capture of Kazan. Sixteenth-century miniature.

43

Sixteenth-century street scene in Moscow, showing a lady's carriage. Woodcut.

and military reforms, the latter including a long overdue modification of the system whereby field commands were assigned on the basis of ancestral family precedence rather than of military competence. It was also at this time that the first rudimentary Russian standing army was established. The units concerned were the *streltsy*, infantry equipped with firearms and retained in permanent garrisons – by contrast with the temporary levies on which Russian military effort had hitherto depended. Other constructive achievements included the introduction of printing (1563).

The death of the Tsaritsa Anastasia in 1560 heralded a marked change in Ivan's attitudes. It was now that he gradually began to earn the title of 'the Terrible', among his early victims being Sylvester and Adashev, whom he imprisoned or banished. One reason for their disgrace was probably a difference of opinion over military policy. The two advisers had wished to follow the conquest of Kazan and Astrakhan with further campaigns against the Tatars, proposing to attack the powerful Crimean Khanate, whereas the Tsar wished to revive an ambition of his grandfather's by extending his territories on the Baltic coast. Ivan's aim was to obtain easier access to western Europe, and in 1558 he

Stephen Batory, King of
Poland (reigned 1575–86).
Contemporary engraving.

accordingly mounted a campaign in the area of modern Estonia and Latvia by
attacking the Livonian Order of Knights, his weakest enemies in the west. But
though the Tsar won some spectacular early victories against the enfeebled Order,
he also aroused the fears of Sweden as well as of Poland-Lithuania. Ivan continued for a quarter of a century, stubbornly and with decreasing success, to
prosecute his futile drive against Sweden and Poland, after they had divided up
between them the lands of the now defunct Livonian Order. Defeated, eventually, by the newly elected Polish King, Stephen Batory, Ivan was forced to make
peace in 1582–83. He now yielded even those territories on the Ingrian coast
which had accrued to Muscovy in his grandfather's reign, retaining only the
mouth of the Neva. Ivan's war in the north-west was a failure as disastrous as his
early victories over the Tatars had been glorious, while also pointing the way to
the future by pursuing ambitions which were to be realized many years later
under Peter the Great.

Contemporary English observers have provided confirmatory evidence of
the terrifying devastation inflicted on Muscovy by Ivan's later policies, as also of
the comparative prosperity of his early reign. In 1553 the explorer Richard

45

Left: Woodcut portrait of Ivan the Terrible by a contemporary artist. *Right:* Russian grant of privilege to a British merchant (Rowland Howard) by Tsar Theodore I (reigned 1584–98).

Chancellor had set sail from Gravesend and landed near the mouth of the Northern Dvina, thus pioneering a new trade route which led to the founding of Archangel thirty years later. Making his way to Moscow, Chancellor was welcomed by the Tsar, who granted the English extensive trading concessions, inspired partly by a hope of inveigling them into an anti-Polish military alliance. In this Ivan was unsuccessful (as also in his later attempts to marry Queen Elizabeth's kinswoman Lady Mary Hastings, though himself married at the time to his fifth or seventh bride). When passing through Muscovy in the early period of Ivan's reign, Chancellor had been struck by the country's size and prosperity. He found Moscow to be a city larger than London. With regard to rural conditions, Chancellor remarked that 'the countrey betwixt [Yaroslavl and Moscow] is very wel replenished with smal Villages, which are so wel filled with people that it is a wonder to see them'. In 1588, however, a later English visitor, Giles Fletcher, found this same countryside 'vacant and desolate without any inhabitant', adding that 'the like is in all other parts of the realm'.

46

BALTIC SEA

WHITE SEA

Solovetsky Monastery

U R A L

Ob

N. Dvina

N Dvina

L. LADOGA

Vyborg

L. ONEGA

G. OF FINLAND

Beloozero

Veliky Ustyug

Narva Ivangorod

LIVONIA

Pskov

Novgorod

Vologda

Khlynov (Vyatka)

Riga

Torzhok

Yaroslavl

Polotsk

W. Dvina

Tver

Rostov

Suzdal

Volga

Kazan

Vilna

Moscow

KAZAN KHANATE

Smolensk

Tula

Ryazan

Oka

Kama

Minsk

LITHUANIA

Chernigov

Kiev

Dnieper

Dniester

CRIMEAN KHANATE

Don

Volga

Yaik (Ural)

ASTRAKHAN KHANATE

Astrakhan

Azov

OTTOMAN EMPIRE

Bakhchisaray

BLACK SEA

CASPIAN SEA

M O U N T A I N S

| 0 | | 500 Mls |
| 0 | | 800 Kms |

Muscovy at the accession (1533) of Ivan IV (Ivan the Terrible).

Such, as attested by many native and other witnesses also, was the devastation inflicted on Muscovy by its first Tsar, for while waging a long and bloody war against Swedes, Poles and Livonians, he had also been engaged in warfare no less bloody against his own subjects. Ivan's chief instrument in conducting these mysterious persecutions was the Oprichnina, an army of licensed gangsters established in 1565. The Oprichniks formed, in essence, the sovereign's private army, and they amounted eventually to some five or six thousand murderous ruffians carefully picked for their loyalty to his person. Clad in black, riding black horses and carrying special emblems (a dog's head and broom), they were entitled to rob and slaughter non-Oprichniks with impunity. Oprichnina was also the name given to extensive lands, largely in northern Russia, which were now gradually detached from the realm as a whole and assigned to these cut-throats, eventually covering between a third and a half of Muscovy.

Among the outrages inflicted by Oprichniks, the sack of Novgorod in 1570 was the most extensive. The appalling massacre was apparently provoked by

An impression of Moscow, from *Civitates Orbis Terrarum* (1570), by Georg Braun and Frans Hogenberg.

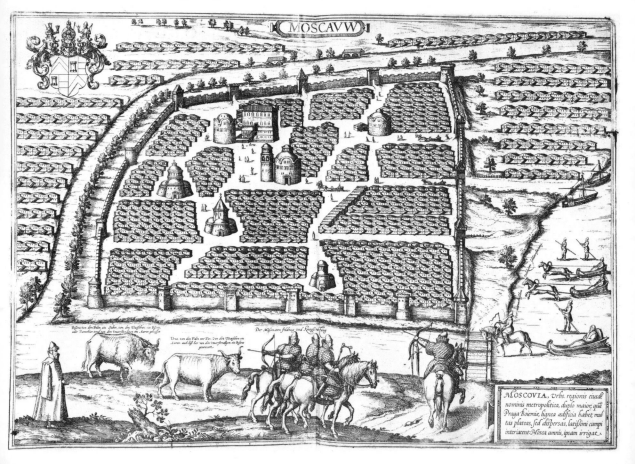

A banquet at Aleksandrovskaya Sloboda, Ivan the Terrible's rural headquarters about sixty miles from Moscow. Seventeenth-century book illustration.

Ivan's groundless fears that this, the second city of his realm, was engaged in betraying him to Poland. Many thousands or possibly tens of thousands of victims were slain in a five-week orgy presided over by the unhinged monarch, who also devastated Tver and other lands on his approach march as well as the countryside surrounding Novgorod itself. Oprichniks tortured and murdered many monks, looting numerous monasteries, besides which the Tsar had two archbishops of Novgorod executed at different times. Nor did he spare the very Metropolitan Philip of Moscow and All Russia, who had dared to denounce Ivan's excesses in public – only to find himself arraigned at a rigged trial before fellow-clerics as a preliminary to being strangled in a monastery cell by the leading Oprichnik, Malyuta ('Babe') Skuratov. Ivan differs from all the other leading later native oppressors of Russia in the extent to which he devised and even personally administered ingenious forms of death, often inflicted before an audience, as in the grim orgy over which he presided in a Moscow square on 25 July 1570, and which included the dismemberment and boiling alive of previously tormented victims. The Tsar was also remarkable in making ostentatiously tearful repentance for his evil deeds, and in assigning sums of money so that prayers might be said for the souls of his mutilated, burnt or drowned victims.

49

Among his many other reported aberrations, the Terrible Tsar is even said to have had an elephant cut to pieces for failing to bow to him.

Directly assaulting his own citizens and also involving them in the abortive Livonian War, Ivan so neglected essential defences at the centre that the Crimean Khan, Devlet-Girey, was able to burn Moscow to the ground in 1571, returning to the south with a huge haul of enslaved captives. So disastrous was the episode that the total Russian casualties were computed at 800,000, a figure which is clearly exaggerated. Be that as it may, Devlet-Girey flung his horsemen against Moscow again in the following year, only to meet decisive defeat by a Russian army under Prince Michael Vorotynsky, a hero of the conquest of Kazan. Ivan later had this same victorious general tortured by fire, personally stoking the flames, for he no doubt found Vorotynsky's warlike prowess inconvenient – as Stalin was to find the military prestige of Marshals Tukhachevsky and Zhukov. Yet this event belongs to the last, and again relatively mild, years of Ivan's reign. So too does the domestic tragedy which occurred when Ivan swung his iron-tipped staff in a fit of temper and struck dead his beloved eldest son and heir, the Tsarevich Ivan Ivanovich – an event which plunged the unhappy father into yet another frenzy of repentance and lamentation.

Unlike many tyrants, Ivan enjoyed an extraordinary degree of popularity among his subjects – perhaps the most mysterious feature in his tantalizing career. Nor has posterity been backward in attempts to explain his perversities as part of a wise and carefully calculated policy. According to an interpretation especially favoured in the Stalin period – when comparisons between the Oprichniks and the Soviet NKVD security police could not fail to occur to the vaguest student of Russian history – the Terrible Tsar's chief aim was to strengthen the centralized Russian state by destroying the boyars, princes and leading churchmen who constituted the chief rivals to the monarchy. This theory has the Tsar allying himself with the minor gentry in order to squeeze out the princes and boyars, who still retained traditional pretensions to grandeur. The Oprichnina, chief instrument in strengthening authoritarian control, was therefore officially described as a 'progressive' phenomenon in the outstandingly authoritarian Stalin era. Stalin himself went even further, once remarking – perhaps as a grimly ironical joke – that Ivan had wrongly wasted time over his prayers which might have been better spent slaughtering yet more boyars.

Though it is indeed true that Ivan sponsored the execution of many great nobles by members of the minor gentry, he also operated in the opposite direction, for many of the minor gentry also became his victims, while princes and boyars

Entrance to the *terem* (women's quarters) in the Moscow Kremlin.

were included among those recruited into the Oprichnina – as also were foreigners resident in Russia. Naturally enough, the Tsar's most numerous victims were found among the common people. As already noted, there was a tendency to idolize the tyrant, but even those who admired him most were well advised to do so from a safe distance. Peasants and petty townsmen accordingly fled from the persecution in their thousands, establishing themselves in the wild lands on the periphery of the south and south-east, where such freedom-seekers and fugitives from centralized terror had now become known as Cossacks.

Terror, taxation and war were not the only reasons for this massive exodus from the centre and north-west of Muscovy. There was also the progressive enserfment of the peasantry, virtually bound to the soil by the end of the century through enactments curtailing the traditional freedom to leave a master's service at the time of St George's Day (26 November) each year. As this development indicates, late sixteenth-century Russia was rapidly evolving into a community where all, from great landowner down to meanest peasant, were becoming members of a service state and subject to the merest whims of their Tsar or of intermediary absolute masters.

Tsar Boris Godunov (reigned
1598–1605). Contemporary portrait.

THE TIME OF TROUBLES

Ivan the Terrible's death in 1584 brought immediate relief to a country demoralized by his maniac caprices, especially as his son and successor, Theodore I,
was a simple-minded, inert creature. The fanatical despot's smouldering glare
now gave way to a harmless imbecile's fixed grin, and the two sovereigns
accordingly exemplify a tendency – many times illustrated in later centuries – for
Russian rulers to be polarized into one of two contrasting types. They tended,
that is, to be either extremely meek or extremely self-assertive, in which respects
they strangely foreshadow the characters in Dostoyevsky's novels.

Excessive passivity in a sovereign often creates around the throne a power
vacuum liable to be filled by some more forceful individual, and in Theodore's
case this role was taken by his brother-in-law Boris Godunov, an energetic and
ambitious former Oprichnik. Though Godunov's style of leadership was more
modern – that is, more cunningly flexible and less savagely erratic – than Ivan's,
he by no means reversed all the policies pursued under the previous Tsar. He
continued to suppress boyar pretensions such as menaced his personal position,
while encouraging the minor gentry, binding the peasants yet more closely to the
soil, and sponsoring the continued penetration of Siberia. Godunov, too, waged

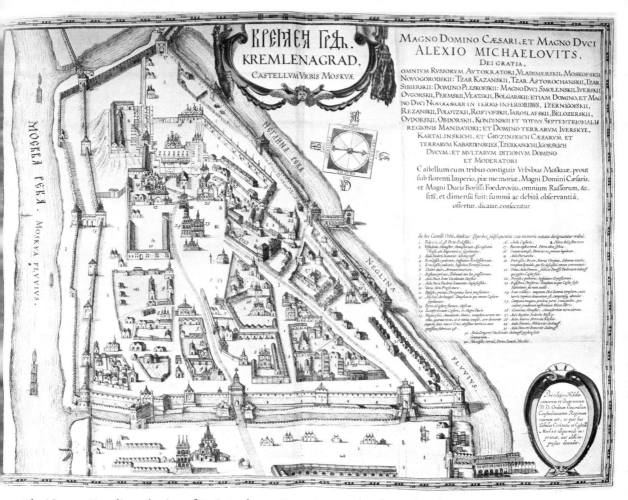

The Moscow Kremlin at the time of Boris Godunov. From *Cosmographie Blaviane* (1663), by Jan Blaeu.

war in the north-west, but succeeded where Ivan had failed when a Muscovite army defeated the Swedes and recovered lands on the southern Baltic coast which had been lost by the Terrible Tsar through his calamitous Livonian War. Again by contrast with Ivan – that great hounder of clerics – Godunov's government much enhanced the prestige of the Orthodox Church in 1589, when the chief Russian prelate was promoted from the secondary grade of metropolitan to the supreme rank of patriarch, which had hitherto been confined to non-Russian branches of Orthodoxy. Job, the first Russian patriarch, was an ally of Godunov's, and the new rank continued in force until left in abeyance by Peter the Great, being later revived in the Soviet period. Favouring contacts with the West, Godunov also arranged for eighteen young Russians to pursue their education abroad.

53

Dying in 1598, Tsar Theodore left no heir. He thereby brought to an abrupt end the line of Prince Daniel which had provided Moscow with rulers for more than three centuries, this line itself being reckoned only part of the ancient Ryurikid dynasty, which traced its origin back to the ninth century. Theodore's failure to provide a successor was an important factor in provoking the Time of Troubles (1605–13), which was to rock the very foundations of Muscovy. Not that this prospect was at first evident when Boris Godunov agreed, with a great parade of reluctance, to accept the throne himself, urged to do so by his ally, the Patriarch Job. But unfortunately for Tsar Boris his reign was plagued by three successive disastrous crop failures, leading to widespread famine in the years 1601–03. Nor was the new Tsar's status by any means secure, for the age expected its rulers to possess genealogical prestige such as he wholly lacked. Godunov thus became vulnerable to attack by the first of the many pretenders to the throne who were to become the curse of seventeenth- and eighteenth-century Russia.

Tsars and Pretenders during the Time of Troubles

Boris Godunov (1598–1605)

Theodore II Godunov (1605)

False Dmitry I (1605–06)

Vasily IV Shuysky (1606–10)

False Dmitry II (1607–10)

Wladyslaw of Poland, Tsar-elect (1610–13)

Known to history as False Dmitry I, the young man in question claimed – and probably believed – himself to be the Tsarevich Dmitry, son of Ivan the Terrible by his last Tsaritsa, and half-brother to Tsar Theodore. The boy had been banished with his mother to the provincial town of Uglich on Ivan the Terrible's death. On 15 May 1591, at the age of nine, he was found with his throat cut in the courtyard of his residence, thus providing Russian history with one of the most notable among its many unsolved murder mysteries. Was the boy slain – as claimed in Pushkin's play, *Boris Godunov*, and Musorgsky's opera of the same name – on Godunov's orders? Or did he perish by a self-inflicted wound, having cut himself with a knife in the course of an epileptic fit – as a commission of inquiry most implausibly reported shortly after the event? Or was some other

The murder of the Tsarevich Dmitry at Uglich in 1591. Seventeenth-century panel.

child the victim, and did the real Dmitry survive to become 'False Dmitry'? Even this last, least likely, possibility is not scouted by all responsible historians. Whatever the Pretender's true identity may have been, he was in any case able to gather an army of Poles and disaffected Cossacks, and he marched on Moscow in spring 1605. Then Tsar Boris suddenly died and the Pretender was able to occupy the capital and to have himself proclaimed Tsar. During his brief rule, lasting less than a year, False Dmitry showed considerable initiative, refusing to act as a mere tool of Poland and spearhead of Catholic penetration into Russia: the role for which his Polish sponsors had groomed him. But he fell victim to a *coup* mounted by disgruntled boyars under Prince Vasily Shuysky, the prime intriguer of the period, after which Shuysky himself was proclaimed Tsar.

By now the Time of Troubles was well under way. This was a period of atrocious suffering, and of devastation comparable in scale to that of the Tatar oppressions, the Civil War of 1918–21, the great Stalinist terror and the Hitlerite invasion of 1941. Many competing anarchic forces now ran riot as huge bands of famished, armed peasants and Cossacks scoured the country, looting, massacring and raping. In 1606 a rebel peasant army under Ivan Bolotnikov marched on Moscow, but was defeated. By now False Dmitry had been followed by a whole crop of other pretenders great and small, but it was a second False Dmitry who became the most prominent among the various spurious Ivans, Gabriels, Martins, Yeroshkas and the like. Posing both as the original Tsarevich Dmitry and as the False Dmitry deposed in 1606, this adventurer established a rival government in the village of Tushino near Moscow, but was eventually murdered. Vasily Shuysky was deposed by *coup d'état*, after which the Swedes (invited) and the Poles (uninvited) began to intervene and seize Russian territory. For three years (1610–12) the Moscow Kremlin was held by a Polish garrison, while a Polish prince, Wladyslaw, enjoyed the status of Tsar-elect – until finally the forces of Russian patriotism, from which neither Church, boyars, gentry, Cossacks nor bonded peasants were immune, asserted themselves against the monstrosity of rule by hated Catholic aliens. Recruiting propaganda sent out by the Patriarch Hermogenes now combined with the organizational talents of a Nizhny Novgorod merchant, Kuzma Minin, and the generalship of a

A Grand Prince of Moscow and a Tatar Great Khan. Seventeenth-century engraving.

Easter procession in the Moscow Kremlin. From De Wicquefort's translation (1719) of the *Voyages* (1656) of Adam Olearius.

prince, Dmitry Pozharsky, to generate a national revival. A Russian army, assembled at Yaroslavl on the upper Volga, marched on Moscow and threw out the Poles, who nevertheless retained a large area of Russian territory in the west, including Smolensk. The Swedes, too, annexed extensive lands in the north-west, now depriving Russia of all access to the Baltic.

During these appalling years Russians received innumerable lessons in the disadvantages of anarchy and chaos. So destructive were the Troubles that the population may have been reduced by over a third, from about fourteen million to nine million, though such figures are very largely guesswork. Moscow and many other towns had been burned and pillaged, while famine and disease had taken a fantastic toll of life. Was all this an object lesson in the advantages of absolute rule by a single unchallenged sovereign? From the eagerness with which the country embraced autocracy again after the Troubles were over,

The installation of
Philaret (the father of
Tsar Michael
Romanov) as
Patriarch of
Moscow.
Seventeenth-century
miniature.

such would appear to have been the collective conclusion drawn by all forces in society: Church, gentry, townsfolk and possibly also the downtrodden peasants, who were always the chief sufferers in Russian upheavals – and may even have preferred the evils of serfdom to the starvation and massacres of the troubled years.

Be that as it may, the quest for a new absolute ruler began in earnest after the Poles had been driven out of Moscow. In February 1613 a new Tsar, Michael Romanov, was chosen after much bargaining by a Land Assembly (*zemsky sobor*) consisting of representatives from various social classes. Though Michael's genealogical claims were not impressive, they were at least stronger than Boris Godunov's, and the dynasty thus founded was to last over three hundred years until extinguished by the February Revolution of 1917 and the abdication of the last Romanov Tsar-Emperor, Nicholas II.

After 1613 the Russian seventeenth century enters a comparatively becalmed area separating the Time of Troubles from the reign of Peter the Great. Not that this was by any means an uneventful interval, for it saw the continued successful development of Muscovite autocratic absolutism: an amazing phenomenon when one considers how poorly the early Romanov rulers seemed equipped by nature to preside over the process. All five of the pre-imperial Romanov Tsars happened to come to the throne as mere striplings. The first in line, Michael, was only sixteen years of age when elected monarch in 1613. Succeeding in 1645, also at the age of sixteen, Michael's son Alexis was followed in 1676 by his eldest son, the fourteen-year-old Theodore III. Then Theodore's brief rule gave way in turn to the joint reign (in 1682) of two juvenile co-Tsars: Theodore's surviving brother Ivan V (aged fifteen) and half-brother Peter I (aged nine), whose elder sister Sophia became regent until 1689.

With the marked exception of Peter I – the infant Peter the Great, whose full potentialities did not become evident until the last decade of the century – none of these sovereigns had been equipped by nature to found an empire. They lacked that aggressive, power-building instinct so evident in the two main architects of earlier independent Muscovy: the Ivans, Great and Terrible. By contrast with those potent figures even the least flaccid of the early Romanov Tsars, Alexis, was known and beloved under the nickname 'Most Gentle'. Tsars Michael and Theodore III were gentler still, both being invalids and reputedly suffering from an ailment of the legs which made it necessary to lift them on to their thrones and sledges, while Ivan V, co-Tsar to the infant Peter, was mentally afflicted. That the bounds of Muscovy should have been drawn ever wider, and that the power of the centralized state should have been still further extended, under a succession of sovereigns so feeble and passive, argues the presence in the Russian people of an elemental urge towards expansion, combined with a willingness to tolerate – to demand, almost – autocratic rule by monarchs whose natural postures were anything but authoritarian. No doubt, however, the very weakness of these Tsars helped to reconcile the people to the further reinforcement of absolute rule. Eased into the shackles of ever-increasing authoritarianism by a succession of masters so kindly, Muscovites were to be utterly taken aback when the ferociously dynamic Peter came of age and exploited to the full the vast powers so casually assumed by his passive predecessors.

Meanwhile Peter's predecessors on the Romanov throne seemed to be living out much of their lives in a charmed dream, blissfully unaware of what the future

MOSCVA

Moscow in the early seventeenth century. From Merian's *Atlas Geographicus et Topographicus* (1643).

Michael (reigned 1613–45),
the first Romanov Tsar.

Tsar Alexis (reigned 1645–76).
Portrait by S. Loputsky (1657).

Tsar Theodore III (reigned 1676–82).
Portrait by B. Saltanov.

Tsar Ivan V, joint sovereign (1682–96) with
Peter the Great.

Stenka Razin (d. 1671), leader of the great Cossack revolt. Contemporary portrait.

might hold. They spent many hours of the day on their feet, robed in heavy, stiff, jewel-encrusted vestments, as they patiently submitted to the exacting rituals of the Orthodox Church. They kept the rigorous prescribed fasts, they received foreign diplomats with lavish ceremonial. Yet, calm and untroubled as this atmosphere may have seemed, it was only one aspect of the seventeenth-century scene, for not all was decorum in the early Romanovite Kremlin. Even the saintly Alexis was liable to box his boyars' ears from time to time, while the boyars themselves were apt to indulge in punch-ups on occasion. This was also an age of continuing cruel punishments, as when one unfortunate individual suffered the judicial amputation of a foot and hand for accidentally firing a gun near the Most Gentle Tsar's palace while hunting jackdaws. In the world beyond the palace there were many riots and rebellions of townsfolk, peasants, Cossacks and even monks – upheavals often quelled by public torture and execution through strappado, knout, burning, beheading, quartering and the like. The most serious of all internal seventeenth-century upheavals was the great Cossack rebellion of Stenka Razin. This engulfed the lower and middle Volga, being suppressed with difficulty by the Tsar's army, after which fellow-Cossacks handed over the leader – who was executed by quartering in Moscow's Red Square in June 1671.

Bogdan Khmelnitsky (1593–1657), the
Ukrainian leader. Engraving by
William Hondius (1651).

Of the seventeenth-century Tsars' pacific temper, and of their reluctance to
extend their frontiers, the Azov episode provides an example. The Turkish
fortress of this name, which gave access to the Sea of Azov and hence to the Black
Sea, was captured by Don Cossacks (still virtually independent of Moscow) in
1637 and held against Turkish attack for four years. Since the Cossacks could
not hope to maintain Azov indefinitely against the Sultan's forces, they offered
to hand it over to Tsar Michael. But the Tsar declined, not wishing to become
embroiled in war with Turkey.

A similar desire to keep the peace made the first two Romanov Tsars reluctant to incorporate the Ukraine, now ruled by Poland, in their territory, despite
overtures in this direction from the (Orthodox) Ukrainians, who preferred
union with their Muscovite co-religionists to rule by alien Catholics. Less
timorous than in the case of Azov, Moscow did eventually decide after much
hesitation to accept the union offered by the Ukrainian leader Bogdan Khmelnitsky, an agreement to this effect being signed in 1654. When the inevitable
war with Poland followed, the Russians managed to avenge their previous
humiliations by defeating their western neighbour. Under the Armistice of
Andrusovo (1667) Moscow acquired substantial territories from Poland,
including Smolensk and the whole of the Ukraine on the left bank of the

Dnieper. Muscovy also acquired Kiev at this time, thus at last taking over the ancient Rus capital. In keeping with his enhanced prestige, Alexis had assumed the title 'Tsar of All Great, Little and White Russia' during the Polish war, thereby adding both the Ukraine (Little Russia) and Belorussia (White Russia) to the domains which he claimed as his own. But though Belorussia was indeed overrun by victorious Muscovite troops during the war, Moscow handed it back under the armistice terms of 1667, and it was to remain under Polish rule for a century and more.

The seventeenth century also saw the penetration of the whole of Siberia, up to the Sea of Okhotsk and the far north-east, by Cossack frontiersmen, one motive for this expansion being the lucrative fur trade. Sparsely populated by primitive tribes, the huge area offered little resistance. It was not occupied as a whole by Russians, but extensively colonized in many isolated settlements, among which Yakutsk, Okhotsk and Irkutsk were added to centres set up in western Siberia in the late sixteenth century. By 1700 Russian settlers east of the Urals numbered about 200,000. Serious resistance to their encroachments was encountered only along the Amur River in the south, where the pioneers came into conflict with the Chinese Manchu Empire. By the Russo-Chinese Treaty of Nerchinsk (1689) this frontier was regulated so effectively that it remained unchanged for a century and a half.

A Dutch embassy enters Moscow in 1665. Seventeenth-century engraving.

So much for external expansion to west and east. With regard to the further internal strengthening of the autocracy, a decline must be noted in the influence of two traditional institutions which had hitherto acted, albeit to a disputed and limited degree, as rival power centres to the monarchy. One of these was the Land Assembly. Such assemblies, which included representatives of various social classes, and were periodically convoked to deal with specific problems, became most useful and important at times of dynastic crisis. A Land Assembly had established Boris Godunov on the throne in 1598, while another – the most important in the institution's history – had elected Michael Romanov as Tsar in 1613. It was a Land Assembly, too, which later recommended the refusal of the Don Cossacks' offer of Azov in 1641, while yet another supported union with the Ukraine in 1654, as described above. Though the Assembly's functions were advisory, except at times of interregnum, its advice carried considerable weight, as the Azov and Ukrainian episodes show. Consultative, too, was a smaller body, the Boyar Duma – successor to a more ancient institution bearing the same name, which had functioned in the Kievan era. This also lost most of its limited powers by the end of the seventeenth century. Another landmark in the concentration of power occurred when the institution of precedence, whereby individuals could claim offices of state on genealogical grounds, was finally abolished in 1682. The record books concerned were burnt, which

The Tsaritsa Natalia, second wife of Tsar Alexis, driving out in state. From Palmkvist's *Album* (1674).

meant the removal of the last remaining barrier hindering the monarch from appointing whomever he wished to offices of state.

In 1649 a new law code was issued. Printed in an edition of two thousand copies, it obtained wider distribution, and in more reliable form, than earlier codes. Among other provisions, it sanctified a procedure already followed in practice by laying down capital punishment as the penalty for treason, attempted treason and failure to denounce treason, thus placing political crime in the Russian statute-book for the first time. The same law code also completed the process of peasant enserfment by extending indefinitely the period – previously subject to a statutory time limit – within which a landlord could recover fugitive peasants.

Seventeenth-century Muscovy was an outstandingly devout realm in which the Church remained a powerful institution, two leading prelates in particular acquiring extensive political powers. The first was the Patriarch Philaret (Theodore Romanov), who also happened to be the father of Michael, the first Romanov Tsar, and who became *de facto* ruler of Muscovy from 1619 until his death in 1633, even assuming the title 'great sovereign', also held by his crowned son. Yet more dominant, not to say domineering, was the low-born Patriarch Nikon, who also termed himself 'great sovereign', persistently humiliating and bullying the kindly Tsar Alexis in the middle years of the century. But there were limits beyond which the Most Gentle sovereign would not abase himself before this arrogant pontiff, who at one point even went on strike, withdrawing from Moscow and refusing to perform his patriarchal functions in an attempt to bring Alexis to heel. Patient though the Gentle Tsar was, such tantrums proved ineffectual in the long run, Nikon being deposed from office and banished to a distant monastery by a conclave of prelates. Thus ended the only serious attempt ever made by the Muscovite Church to assert itself over the temporal power. That the easy-going Alexis should have emerged victorious in a duel with so formidable and assertive an opponent is a measure of the innate strength of the seventeenth-century autocracy as an institution.

Though Nikon fell from power as an individual, the important ecclesiastical reforms sponsored by this turbulent patriarch remained in force. They included a revision of the Russian scriptural and liturgical texts through collation with the Greek originals from which they had come to diverge over the centuries. They also included such apparently trivial rulings as those determining the number of fingers which believers should hold together as they crossed themselves, the precise spelling of the name Jesus and the conditions governing the use of the

The bell tower of Ivan the Great in the Moscow Kremlin. From De Wicquefort's translation (1719) of the *Voyages* (1656) of Adam Olearius.

word Alleluia. In so pious an age these matters assumed immense importance, and many of the faithful indignantly refused to accept Nikon's tinkering with the cult of their fathers, thus inaugurating a schism in the Church and becoming known as Old Believers. Their most remarkable representative was the Arch-priest Avvakum, author of an autobiography in the Russian vernacular which is an important literary landmark. The Old Believers were severely persecuted by the state, Avvakum himself being burnt at the stake. Other schismatics staged protest demonstrations of a special kind by immolating themselves *en masse* in wooden churches and barns. Restricted very largely to Great Russians (as opposed to Ukrainians and Belorussians), and mainly confined to peasants, lower townsfolk and merchants, the Old Belief movement expressed Russian traditionalism and hostility to foreign-based innovations. Despite persecutions continuing through the Imperial and Soviet periods, the movement is still far from extinct in the officially atheist revolutionary state.

Owing to Peter the Great's policy of importing European institutions and customs wholesale, students of earlier Russian history have sometimes tended to underrate the process whereby seventeenth-century Muscovy was progressively assimilating European influences long before its principal europeanizer began operations. Some Russian historians, by contrast, have been a little over-zealous in redressing the balance. As they are quick to point out, even in Tsar Michael's reign the army was already being remodelled on foreign patterns with the aid of mercenary officers from western Europe. Foreigners helped to establish the infant Russian theatre, while the study of Polish and Latin – though not yet to any great degree of the major modern European languages – became fashionable. Commerce with the West, too, so increased that a special enclave – termed the German Quarter, but intended for all western Europeans – was set up in Moscow and included its own Protestant churches, churches of the suspect Catholic faith not being permitted. Foreigners, then, were welcome in seventeenth-century Muscovy, but within limits, being quarantined lest they contaminate the Orthodox. Yet despite all suspicion, xenophobia, danger and discomforts, they continued to flock to Muscovy and to practise their trades or professions. Tsar Alexis's personal physician, to name only one individual, was the Englishman Samuel Collins, whose memoirs form a fascinating item in the fast-growing corpus of alien reminiscences of Russia. Since Russia-based Russians had long been learning the unwisdom of committing their views and experiences to paper, foreigners such as Collins – and also defectors from Muscovy such as Gregory Kotoshikhin and Ivan the Terrible's enemy Prince Kurbsky – have provided a substantial proportion of the primary historical sources from the sixteenth century onwards.

Though foreign visitors had begun the discovery or rediscovery of Russia in the late fifteenth century, at the time when Columbus discovered America, the country still continued to make a strange and puzzling impression two centuries later. Then – as also now, in the late twentieth century – Russia often impressed foreign visitors as quaint, whether engagingly or barbarously so. A Christian society, even if of the unfamiliar eastern variety, and peopled by many individuals of more or less western facial appearance, the Tsar's realm yet made a weird impact. It was full of onion-domed churches, the endless din of bells and the corpses of publicly tortured felons. Its dignitaries wore long beards and flowing oriental robes, practising the kow-tow and keeping their women in purdah, though such Tatar fashions were already declining in the late seventeenth century.

Did these oddities belong properly to east or west? Neither the foreign visitors, themselves no mean oddity to their Russian hosts, nor the Russians themselves have ever been able to form a definitive consensus on this central problem of Russian history.

PETER THE GREAT

Chosen Tsar in 1682, Peter the Great was to make a more violent impact on pre-revolutionary Russia than any other single individual by his superhuman efforts to convert old-fashioned Muscovy into a modern European state.

So momentous a prospect did not appear in the least likely when Peter's accession as a nine-year-old boy provoked the first dynastic crisis of the Romanov line. After Theodore III's death, the throne would naturally have reverted to his elder surviving brother, the fifteen-year-old Ivan, had not Ivan been so obviously feeble in mind and body. This being the case, the Patriarch called various notables to a scratch gathering sometimes rated as a Land Assembly, and it was this body which proclaimed the precocious, robust and mentally alert Peter as sovereign. But then, two weeks later, the *streltsy* – the soldier-traders, largely of Old Believer persuasion, who garrisoned Moscow – raised a revolt, marched on the Kremlin with banners waving and embarked on a three-day massacre of Peter's uncles and of his other associates on his mother's side. The *streltsy* spared Peter himself and his mother, while elevating Ivan to the position of co-Tsar – but with senior status – alongside Peter. Peter's half-sister Sophia then became regent. After witnessing horrors more traumatic than those which beset the infant Ivan the Terrible, Peter conceived a loathing for Moscow, and for the *streltsy* in particular, which later prompted a terrible vengeance.

By 1689 the Regent Sophia was showing signs of intending to oust her two brothers and assume the role of autocrat herself, whereupon Peter's supporters overthrew her by *coup d'état* and confined her in a convent. After the removal of this obstacle, the seventeen-year-old youth did not immediately grasp power, but left affairs of state to his mother and her advisers, his own energies being taken up with continued apprenticeship in the arts of war. He had begun by playing at soldiers with boys of his own age in a series of military games which became ever more earnest as he drilled his young companions into the nucleus of two future guards regiments: the Preobrazhensky and Semyonovsky.

Medal struck in honour of the birth of Peter the Great in 1672.

Fascinated also by boats and ship-building, he extended this interest with similar enthusiasm, visiting Archangel (as yet Russia's only port) in 1693–94 and sailing the White Sea. Such were the youthful pastimes of the future founder of the Russian navy and creator of the first effective Russian regular army.

Peter's ferocious energy was combined with the intensely practical bent of one who must build everything with his own hands. He became a skilled shipwright and master of a dozen other trades, working for long hours at these activities. Yet Russia's most industrious apprentice was also a drunken hooligan who strangely combined religious piety with ridicule of Orthodox practices through blasphemous buffooneries staged by himself and his tipsy companions. Early married off by his mother to an old-fashioned Muscovite girl, the young Tsar duly sired an heir, but wedlock signally failed to steady him. He preferred the company of a German mistress, Anna Mons. He also shocked old-fashioned Muscovites by frequenting Moscow's German Quarter, where such heretic associates as General Patrick Gordon (a Scot in Russian service) and the Swiss adventurer Franz Lefort became allies, tutors or boon companions. The young man's orgies were rendered all the more terrifying by his gigantic stature and great physical strength, combined with a nervous spasm which afflicted his face and neck.

Eudoxia Lopukhin, the first wife of Peter the Great. Engraving (*c.* 1810).

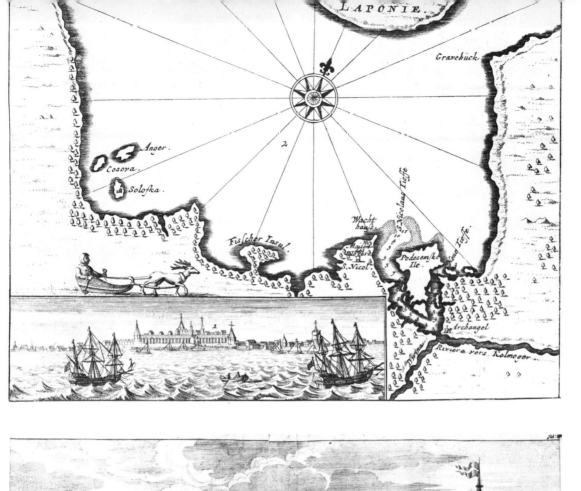

LAPONIE.

Gravchück

Anger
Cosova
Solofka

Fifcher Insul

Wacht haus
Maison
S. Nicol.

S. Nicolaus Tieffe

Podesemske Ile

Archangel

Dvina Riviere vers Kolmogor

Equipping himself rapidly for the role of autocrat, the Tsar found cares of state thrust upon him by his mother's death in 1694, as also – at least formally – by the death of his half-brother and co-Tsar Ivan V two years later. Meanwhile Peter had helped to mount an unsuccessful military expedition against the southern fortress of Azov, still held by the Turks. Defeated in 1695, he showed characteristic resilience by immediately building a new fleet (partly with his own axe), sailing it down the Don and capturing Azov in the following year.

In 1697–98 the young Tsar crowned his multiple apprenticeship with an eighteen-month Great Embassy to western Europe which he accompanied – incognito, but recognized by all and sundry – under the name of Peter Mikhaylov. This excursion took him to the Swedish-held Baltic coast, Germany, Holland, England and Austria on a working tour of inspection which led to the recruitment of many foreign specialists for service in Russia, while the sovereign himself continued his own education and carousals with unabated energy.

Peter the Great meets the Viennese embassy at the gates of Moscow, 1698. From J.G. Korb, *Diarium Itineris in Moscoviam* (1700). *Right:* Kneller's portrait of Peter the Great, painted in England in 1698.

73

Having by now fully embraced his vocation as Muscovy's future euro-peanizer, Peter was surprised in Vienna by news that the hated *streltsy* – symbols of Old Russia – had again raised a revolt at home. Though this was quickly quelled by Peter's deputies, he reopened the case after returning post haste to his capital. He had over a thousand *streltsy* executed after ordeal by strappado, knout and fire – a process designed to investigate the complicity of the nun and former regent Sophia. She was found to have encouraged the affair and was placed under closer guard, while the bodies of three executed *streltsy* were strung up outside her cell window. On Peter's orders hundreds of other rebel corpses were also left dangling from their gallows, and festooned the terrorized capital for months. He thus made it clear that Muscovy had a real master at last – one who meant to make full use of the autocratic powers which had so casually fallen to his inert predecessors.

As a further symbol of his determination to haul Muscovy kicking and screaming into the eighteenth century, the Tsar refused to let his boyars kow-tow to him in traditional oriental style, and took scissors, cutting off their beards and snipping the capacious sleeves of their traditional robes as a prelude to making shaven chins and European dress obligatory for all Russian gentry and officials. Along with robes and beards, the ancient title of boyar was soon to disappear as well. Peter also greeted the eighteenth century by adopting the Julian Calendar,

The assassination of Artamon Matveyev (former guardian of Peter the Great's mother, the Tsaritsa Natalia) during the *streltsy* mutiny of 1682. From P. Krekshin, *Life of Peter the Great*.

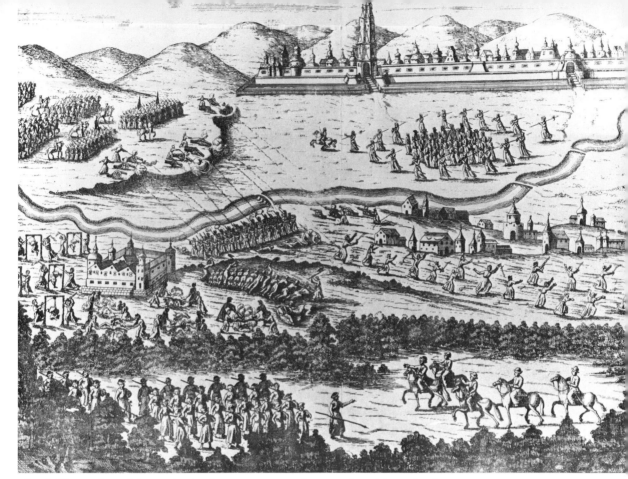

The rebellious *streltsy* fighting against loyal Russian troops under General Patrick Gordon during the mutiny of 1698. From J. G. Korb, *Diarium Itineris in Moscoviam* (1700).

an important symbolic change since Muscovy had hitherto reckoned time from the notional beginning of the world. For so backward a state to have been, as it were, 6,508 years ahead of western Europe was absurd, and the Julian Calendar put it, more appropriately, eleven days in arrears.

As a means of breaking through to western Europe, Peter determined to conquer an extensive section of the Baltic coast, an ancestral Russian ambition pursued sporadically since the days of Ivan III. The Tsar thus became embroiled in his long but victorious Northern War against Sweden. It began with disaster when a small Swedish army under Charles XII defeated the Russians at Narva in 1700, Peter himself having fled from the field on the eve of the battle. He thus conformed with the tradition of military discretion long practised by Muscovite grand princes, but also made himself the laughing-stock of Europe.

Medal issued to commemorate the capture (1704) by the Russians of Narva, the scene of their defeat by the Swedes four years earlier.

The Battle of Lesnaya, 28 September 1708, in which Peter the Great defeated the Swedes – a prelude to his famous victory at Poltava. Early eighteenth-century engraving (detail).

Resilient as ever after his army's rout, he proceeded to rebuild his forces, gaining his main victory over Charles XII at Poltava in 1709. This was one of the most decisive battles in world history, and marked the achievement of permanent Russian supremacy in north-eastern Europe, though the Northern War dragged on until the Peace of Nystad was signed in 1721. Russia thereby annexed Ingria and Karelia, as also the territory of modern Estonia and (partly) of modern Latvia, acquiring the Baltic coastline and hinterland as far down as Riga. The German élite of the Baltic provinces was extensively recruited by Peter and his successors, supplying Russia with many leading generals and administrators who proved no less patriotic – and reputedly more efficient – than native-born Russians.

The Battle of Poltava, in which Peter the Great defeated Charles XII of Sweden on 27 June 1709. Painting by Nattier (detail).

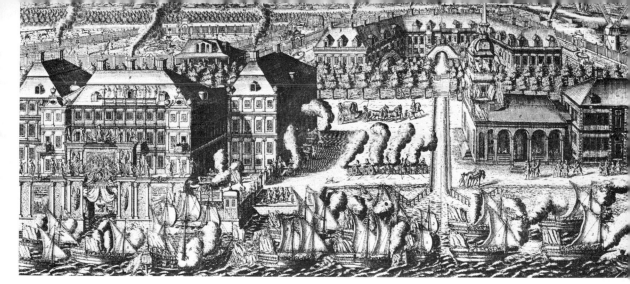

St Petersburg, 1719. Captured Swedish galleys are seen in the foreground. Contemporary engraving by A.F. Zubov.

In 1703 the Tsar had founded a port, St Petersburg – at the mouth of the Neva, on the very edge of his realm and in the heart of the territory which he was disputing with Sweden. In 1712 he made this his capital in place of the hated Moscow. The new city was built by countless dragooned serfs on swamps under appalling conditions, and claimed scores of thousands of victims among its constructors. This was more, perhaps, than the tally of soldiers slain in the Northern War, and possibly as many as died building Stalin's White Sea Canal in 1931–33, another brutally conceived élite project in the Russian tradition. The building of St Petersburg was also a tremendous act of faith, both in Peter's prospects of victory over the Swedes and in the success of his revolutionary attack on the ways of Old Muscovy. As a symbol of the Tsar's eventual triumph, his Senate and Holy Synod (both bodies were his own creations) celebrated the victorious Peace of Nystad by solemnly conferring three new titles on him: 'Father of the Fatherland', 'Emperor of All Russia' and 'Peter the Great'.

Thus, in 1721, the Russian Empire replaced Muscovy and the 'St Petersburg period' of Russian history began. The new city was to remain the capital until 1918, when Moscow reassumed its ancient primacy. St Petersburg carried the name Petrograd from 1914 until 1924 when, by a further change of name, it became Leningrad.

Though Peter's reforms penetrated into innumerable crannies of Russian life, they were not conceived as a whole, many of them being *ad hoc* measures adopted in order to increase the war-waging capacity of a country which

77

The wedding of Peter the Great and Catherine, his second wife, in February 1712. Contemporary engraving by A. F. Zubov.

enjoyed only a few months of peace during its first Emperor's quarter of a century as effective ruler. The establishment of a regular army around the nucleus of two newly formed guards regiments, the Preobrazhensky and Semyonovsky, was one major achievement. Another was the founding of a navy where none had existed before. Typically, the Tsar and future Emperor took a prominent part in drafting the official regulations for both arms of the services. He also helped to build up a merchant fleet, fostering foreign trade, seeking relations with areas as distant as Japan and Madagascar, and encouraging the building of factories, to which serf labourers were consigned in quantity. Local government was extensively though less effectively reformed, the realm being divided into provinces (*gubernii*), an institution which continued in modified form until 1917. So too did the Table of Ranks, a hierarchy of fourteen grades covering civil servants and court officials, as well as naval and military officers.

To manage departments of state, Peter set up colleges on the Swedish model in place of the former loose and cumbrous Offices (*prikazy*) of Muscovy, while the Senate, also an innovation, was to supervise administration as a whole under its Procurator General. As for Church affairs, Peter encouraged the

The library of the Kunstkammer in St Petersburg, founded by Peter the Great and opened in 1719.

secularization of Russia by allowing the powerful office of Patriarch to lapse in 1700 and setting up a new body, the Holy Synod, under a lay administrator (the Chief Procurator) to manage ecclesiastical affairs. He sponsored the publication of the first Russian newspaper, reformed the alphabet, and encouraged the translation of foreign books into Russian – with a characteristic emphasis on works of technical and practical significance. He also fostered education, even forbidding marriage to reluctant scholars among members of his gentry. Taxation was greatly increased and diversified, becoming a grievous burden on a population now conscripted for state service to a degree achieved by no previous Russian ruler. Behind the whole structure lay an apparatus of terror economically administered by Peter's political police, the Preobrazhensky Office: a handful of ruthless clerks who could call in the army's aid when necessary. Thus Russia's remarkable and continuing history as a terrorist bureaucracy effectively began in the pioneering Emperor's reign.

Though Peter's methods were brutal in the extreme, he did not cultivate brutality for its own sake, except of course in the many cases when his unfortunate guests were tormented at the drunken Tsar-Emperor's table as an expression

79

Peter the Great's programme of enlightenment included the sponsoring of the first Russian newspaper and the publication of practical and educational books. *Far left*: Four pages from *Vedomosti* ('news'), of 1722. *Left*: Page from an almanac of 1721, giving advice on days favourable for bloodletting and other medical adventures. *Below*: Pages from children's books; that on the left, from Istomin's ABC, explains the letter 'psi' by illustrations of 'psalter' and 'psalm'.

of his high spirits. Thus the suppressions of the *streltsy*, and later of the Astrakhan mutineers and rebellious Don Cossacks under Bulavin, were more of a
scientifically applied deterrent than were the massacres ordained by Ivan the
Terrible and Stalin. The most notable single rebel of the reign was Peter's son
Alexis, a meek, pious, stooping individual whose main offence in his awesome
father's eyes was an unwillingness or inability to buckle to and learn the business
of a soldier-statesman. Without seeking to head any resistance movement,
Alexis inevitably attracted the hopes of those who revered traditional Muscovy,
often believing Peter to be Anti-Christ, or a changeling foisted on the Kremlin
in infancy by German heretics. Tormented by Peter's demands on him, Alexis
became the most notable of all Russian political defectors when he escaped
to the Holy Roman Empire in 1716, only to be tricked into returning by his
father's agent. Alexis perished in prison, possibly knouted to death. He was in
effect killed by his father – but deliberately and cold-bloodedly, by contrast
with the fit of temper in which Ivan the Terrible had slain his son and heir.

Revolutionary though Peter's reforms were, Russia had – as indicated above
– already begun to assimilate European influences long before his birth. He was,
therefore, by no means charting a new course, but violently wrenching the rudder
in a direction towards which the country was already veering. Another limita-
tion on Peter's impact was his failure to improve the downtrodden status of the
peasants who formed the overwhelming majority of his subjects. These were
pushed further into slavery under the great Tsar-Emperor, who drafted them
en masse to public works and factories, also bestowing them on his favourites by
their tens of thousands. Another dubious legacy was the great cultural rift be-
queathed to Russia by her first Emperor. Resplendent in western gear, jabbering
away in various European languages, his new-style gentry and officials had little
in common with the benighted muzhiks who formed the bulk of the population
and who (together with priests and merchants) continued to maintain antique
Muscovite garb, speech and customs. If, three-quarters of a century after the
first Tsar-Emperor's death, only a small percentage of the Russian population
seemed fitted to enter the nineteenth century, while the rest – largely peasants –
still belonged in spirit to the ninth, Peter must bear much of the responsibility.

In the middle of the nineteenth century the extent and desirability of Peter's
contribution to Russia's development became an endlessly gnawed bone of
contention in the controversy between the Westernizers (who welcomed the
Petrine reforms) and the Slavophils (who deplored them). Neither then nor since
has there been any agreed verdict on the giant Tsar-Emperor's achievements.

Catherine I (reigned 1725–7) being crowned as Tsaritsa by her husband Peter the Great. She succeeded to the throne on his death.

THE AGE OF EMPRESSES

In 1722 Peter the Great presented Russia with her first law of succession to the throne, an ill-conceived measure empowering each ruling sovereign to designate as his heir any person whom he might choose. No provision was, however, made for the event of a monarch dying without naming such a successor. The result was a sequence of dynastic crises, of which the first occurred immediately after Peter's death, when the very author of this unpromising new law turned out to have perished intestate. The succession was, in fact, settled – illegally, and inevitably so in the absence of any prescribed procedure – by a caucus of notables who chose Peter's bawdy and brandy-swilling widow, Catherine I, under threat of intervention on her behalf by officers of the Preobrazhensky and Semyonovsky Guards. Both the accession of a woman as the first female sovereign of Russia in her own right, and the key role played by the Guards, helped to set the pattern for the century's dynastic development as a whole. Guards officers helped to secure autocratic status for the Empress Anne in 1730. Guards officers, too, played a crucial role in obtaining the throne for Elizabeth in 1741, and for Catherine II in 1762.

Left: The Empress Anne (reigned 1730–40). Contemporary engraving. *Right:* The Empress Elizabeth (reigned 1741–61). Contemporary engraving.

Russia's four empresses ruled for two-thirds of a century between them, each being briefly succeeded on her death by an ineffectual male incumbent: a boy (Peter II), a baby (Ivan VI), a politically inept adult (Peter III) and one widely held to be a maniac (Paul I). Since the first of these emperors died of small-pox in his minority, while the other three were all assassinated, this may justly be described as an unlucky epoch for Romanov males. It is a curious fact that only two male Romanovs (Peter III and Paul I) succeeded to the throne as adults between the founding of the dynasty in 1613 and the end of the eighteenth century.

Typically of this showy but indecorous age, its two leading empresses – Elizabeth and Catherine the Great – were both usurpers. The latter was an especially flagrant intruder, for she was of German origin, whereas the estranged spouse whom she ousted (Peter III) was at least a grandson of Peter the Great, ineptly appointed as her successor by Elizabeth – but legally, in so far as this was possible for one who had herself usurped the throne in the first place. The palace revolutions of 1741 and 1762, in which the nocturnal conspiracies of gallant guardees carried attractive and highly sexed youngish princesses to

The palace of Prince Menshikov, favourite of Peter the Great, in St Petersburg. Engraving by A. F. Zubov (*c.* 1720).

power, seem to anticipate – as does so much else in eighteenth-century Russia – the dynastic capers of the fictional Ruritania. As a result of such episodes, the Russian throne – hereditary in practice in the Muscovite era, and decreed appointive by Peter the Great in 1722 – became, as has been well said, purely *occupative* during a period over-endowed with potential Ruperts of Hentzau.

The age of empresses and palace revolutions was also the age of favourites: powerful individuals who owed their positions to personal ascendancy over the sovereign of the time. By no means all favourites were lovers of a reigning empress, though many did enjoy that status. Nor were they all foreigners, despite an impression to this effect which was general among the many Russians who suffered from their caprices. Empress's bedfellow or not, alien or Russian, a favourite was one who exploited his position in order to glut a gross appetite for luxuries, titles and power. The perch was precarious in the extreme, and there was always the danger of being toppled by some younger, better-looking, more reckless intriguer. Among the early favourites Ernst Biron, lover of the Empress Anne, incurred especially widespread loathing. The detestation in which he was held, as were other prominent Germans during Anne's reign, helped to inspire the *coup d'état* which set Elizabeth on the throne. But the

The assassination of Peter III, husband of Catherine the Great, in July 1762. Contemporary engraver's impression.

The coronation of Catherine II (the Great; reigned 1762–96) in the Uspensky Cathedral, Moscow, on 22 September 1762. Engraving of the 1770s.

change of rulers (after the brief, also Teuton-dominated, reign of the infant Ivan VI) merely replaced pro-German with pro-French leanings, while by no means abolishing favouritism as an institution. Catherine the Great, too, had her favourites, among whom Potemkin became outstandingly powerful. It was a rash lover, however, who attempted to dominate the masterful Empress, despite Potemkin's success in doing so – for she was in many respects a true successor to Peter the Great, who had naturally kept all his many protégés and favourites firmly in their place. In her later years Catherine began taking ever younger lovers, her last favourite (the preposterous and foppish Platon Zubov) being indulged in a manner which recalls the indiscretions of earlier rulers – with the result that he conceived ideas far above his ludicrous station.

The eighteenth century witnessed a considerable extension of European Russia's southern and western frontiers, at the expense of Turkey and Poland respectively.

Even Peter the Great had failed against Turkey. Leading an army into Turkish-held Moldavia in 1711, the Tsar had escaped probable capture through the mysterious failure of the commanding Turkish Grand Vizier to spring the trap into which his Russian enemy had marched. After this reprieve, which became known as the Miracle of the Prut, Peter had been forced to return Azov to Turkey. Then, in the war of 1736–39, Russia defeated Turkey, re-covering Azov and annexing part of the southern steppes. Yet the Crimean Tatars (Turkish subjects) were still harrying the Ukraine as late as the middle of the eighteenth century, an irritation well calculated to stimulate continued Russian expansion towards the Black Sea coast. Two further victorious wars against Turkey resulted in Russian annexation of all the southern steppes down to the Black Sea and as far west as the Dniester. These acquisitions included the Crimea itself, seized in 1783. Thus, after nearly five and a half centuries, the Tatar peril was finally extinguished. Christened New Russia, the annexed territories were administered by Catherine's leading satrap, Potemkin, who was created Prince of Tauris and who organized, in 1787, a grandiose six-month tour of inspection by the Empress. During this expedition, which began by specially constructed sledge over the snows of central Russia, the inhabitants of Tula are reported to have lined the road – but to have prostrated themselves with zeal so extreme, when the sumptuous cortège passed by, that none so much as glimpsed the Empress. Then the expedition is found sailing down the Dnieper on a lavishly appointed river fleet while Potemkin points out his famous 'villages': two-dimensional stage props designed to create the illusion of surging

◄ Catherine the Great on horseback. Copied from a painting by Virgilius Erichsen (1762).

Left: Prince G. A. Potemkin of Tauria
(1739–91). Contemporary portrait.

prosperity in the newly colonized lands. But though such instant colonization was not possible even for a Potemkin, the settlement of New Russia proceeded apace, its population increasing fourfold from some 800,000 in 1787 to over three million by 1862. Immigrant German farmers were among those induced to settle in these parts by the Russian government.

While Russia was thus expanding in the south, further annexations were also taking place in the west and involved the destruction of Poland's independence. Already virtually a Russian protectorate, the ravished country was parcelled up in the three successive partitions of 1772, 1793 and 1795. The result was to give Russia her first common frontiers with her fellow-partitioners, Austria and Prussia. These operations incidentally extended the Empire's sway over the whole of Belorussia, while non-Slav areas, Courland and Lithuania, were also numbered among the new annexations. The new citizens acquired by Russia included about a million Jews, who thus entered an empire where the Jewish population had hitherto been relatively insignificant.

The age also witnessed further Russian colonization in Asia, central and far eastern – and, even beyond that area, in North America. A Dane in Russian service, Vitus Bering, led two expeditions to Kamchatka, giving his name to the straits which separate Siberia from Alaska. The pioneering spirit, land hunger and the profits of the fur trade combined to inspire succeeding Russian venturers to penetrate the Aleutian Islands and to turn Alaska into the Russian colony which was eventually (in 1867) sold to the United States.

St Petersburg in the reign of Catherine the Great. View across the River Neva. Engraving by Le Bas (1778).

As mentioned above, Peter the Great had drafted virtually all his subjects into the service of his all-powerful state. The result was that enserfed peasants did at least serve masters who were themselves more or less enserfed in practice, albeit on a comparatively exalted level. Under Peter's successors this situation changed, owing to the progressive emancipation of the gentry from all duties to the state. In 1762 Peter III formally freed gentlemen from any obligations during peace time, and their new privileges were further strengthened in 1785, when Catherine the Great granted the gentry a charter. Themselves exempted from taxation and service obligations, landowning gentlemen became responsible for collecting taxes and for drafting army recruits among their peasantry, and also in effect for policing the countryside. The period when estates had been granted temporarily, and only in respect of service obligations, had long passed, such estates having now become permanent property which an owner could will to his heirs along with the attached serfs. Entitled to buy and sell farm labourers at will, the gentry also received from Catherine punitive powers so extensive that a master's whim was enough to consign an offending peasant to permanent hard labour in Siberia. Knouting and hard labour were prescribed as the punishment for any serf who dared to complain against his owner. The general effect was to reduce the peasant masses to a condition yet more akin to slavery.

Besides becoming more intensive, enserfment was also extended to an ever widening number of victims owing to the monarchs' practice of granting land

A coin struck by the 'government' of the rebel leader Pugachov.

and peasants in enormous quantity to favoured individuals. This procedure had already been followed by Peter the Great, but his successors outdid his efforts, over 1,300,000 male peasants (and their womenfolk) being handed over to private owners between 1740 and 1801. Catherine the Great herself gave away nearly a million peasants of both sexes in this way. Yet she also contrived to pose as an enlightened autocrat imbued with the humanitarian ideals of such contemporaries as Voltaire and Diderot, with whom she eagerly discoursed or maintained correspondence.

Though the eighteenth century saw a further consolidation of the centralized absolutist autocracy, now protected by its corps of newly privileged gentlemen, the downtrodden peasant masses remained by no means quiescent. Nor was one notable seventeenth-century tradition abandoned: that whereby various pretenders periodically challenged the throne. As in earlier and less enlightened days, a pretender leading mutinous Cossacks from the periphery could still pose the gravest danger to the state. One such outbreak in particular attained truly menacing proportions in the eighteenth century: that of Yemelyan Pugachov. Proclaiming himself to be Peter III, who had in fact been murdered by Catherine's minions in 1762, the rebel chieftain alluded to the great Empress as his wife and set up a bogus court modelled on that of St Petersburg. Mean-

Left: Pugachov is taken to Moscow in an iron cage. Contemporary engraving. *Right:* Pugachov and his accomplices await execution in Moscow, 10 January 1775.

A contemporary painting of the Battle of Kinburn (1787) at the mouth of the River Dnieper. The victorious Russians beat off a Turkish attempt to storm their positions.

while his irregular troops were hanging all the landowners on whom they could lay their hands and burning their manors. Surging on from the River Yaik (since renamed Ural), where the rising had originated, to the classic area of revolt under Stenka Razin – the Volga – Pugachov captured Kazan and threatened Moscow in the winter of 1773–74. Eventually regular troops crushed the outbreak, Pugachov being brought in an iron cage to Moscow, where he was beheaded and quartered. His severed limbs were displayed in various parts of the former capital, while savage punitive expeditions crushed the remnants of his rebellion. Such were the methods of Voltaire's most renowned lady disciple when the security of her throne was menaced, though it must be conceded that for Catherine, as for Peter the Great, terror was always a rational means to an end – never an end in itself.

The century saw a further widening of the cultural rift more or less created under Peter the Great, whereby a small, clean-shaven, polite, privileged élite of europeanized French-speaking gentlefolk and officials presided over a mass of

uncouth, bearded, dumb, illiterate, enslaved muzhiks. The cultural achieve/
ments of this élite and its foreign tutors must not be despised. In 1724 the
Academy of Sciences was founded, a brain/child of Peter the Great, and was
followed in 1755 by Russia's first university, that of Moscow. Another achieve/
ment of Elizabeth's reign was the building of St Petersburg's Winter Palace
by the Italian architect Rastrelli. Partly destroyed by fire and reconstructed
under Nicholas I, this ornate and elaborate edifice became the Tsars' main
residence in St Petersburg. It was with the storming of this same building, which
had become the last refuge of the short/lived post/Tsarist Provisional Govern/
ment, that Lenin's Bolsheviks were to crown their seizure of Petrograd (as
the city was then called) in October 1917.

A more sophisticated patroness of the arts than Elizabeth, the Empress
Catherine commissioned many distinguished foreign architects to embellish
her capital. Her agents purchased paintings by Old Masters in western Europe,
and she founded the St Petersburg Hermitage, foremost museum of her day.
Among the works of art commissioned by her is one which still forms a notable
landmark in Leningrad: Falconet's monumental equestrian statue of Peter I,
dedicated to him by Catherine II and mounted on a gigantic rock plinth
specially imported from Finland.

The Academy of Sciences, founded in St Petersburg in 1724 by Peter the Great.

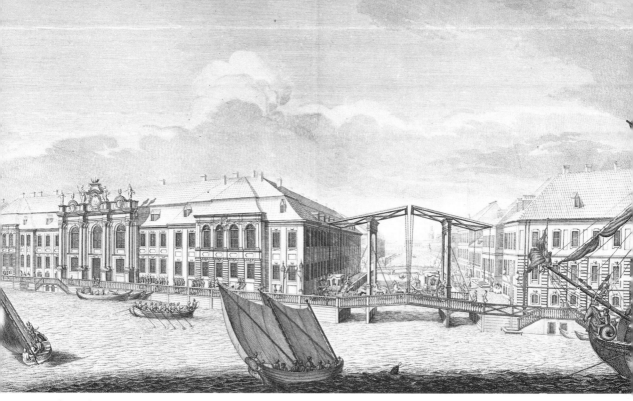

View of the older Winter Palace in St Petersburg and of the Moyka canal, seen across the
River Neva. Eighteenth-century engraving. *Below:* The solemn unveiling, in 1782, of the famous
equestrian statue of Peter the Great in St Petersburg. Dedicated to him by Catherine the Great,
the statue is the work of the French sculptor Falconet. Contemporary engraving.

Copper five-copeck piece
of Catherine the Great,
minted in 1793.

Though the urbane sovereign had light-heartedly quelled the two traditional menaces to her throne, those of palace revolutionaries and Cossack-backed pretenders, she found herself seriously alarmed by a new and very different peril which arose in the last years of her reign and was posed by the French Revolution. It was the French upheaval of 1789, and the subsequent execution of Louis XVI, which first raised a spectre daunting to all the remaining Romanovs and eventually fatal to their line: that of a modern-style revolution. Previous threats to the absolutist Russian throne had, after all, come from individuals who wished to change the ruler rather than the method of rule. The only notable exception to this among the various crises of the eighteenth century had been an abortive attempt by certain noble would-be oligarchs to persuade the Empress Anne to accept certain formal limitations on her power at the time of her accession in 1730. But now, at the end of the century, people were beginning to ask whether an absolutist monarchy could constitute an acceptable form of government in a modern state – particularly when accompanied, as in the Russian Empire, by the virtual enslavement of the overwhelming majority of the population. Such scepticism might eventually prove a greater menace to the fabric of autocracy than peasants' axes. The Empress Catherine accordingly reacted with great ferocity when one of her subjects, Alexander Radishchev, published an outspoken attack on the institutions of autocracy and serfdom, his *Journey from St Petersburg to Moscow* (1790). So seriously was the offence re-garded that Radishchev, often known as the first Russian radical, found himself formally condemned to death, this sentence being eventually commuted by the Empress to exile in Siberia. Another intellectual offender of the period, Nicholas Novikov, was confined to Schlüsselburg Fortress by Voltaire's most illustrious disciple for publishing works antagonistic to the Orthodox Church. Thus began the long duel between the Russian state and dissident writers – a duel which has continued sporadically up to the present day, involving Pushkin, Dostoyevsky, Tolstoy, Gorky, Pasternak and Solzhenitsyn, as well as many other less distinguished authors, in molestation by the Imperial or Soviet political police.

To the long reign of Catherine, both glorious and oppressive in so many ways, the brief rule (1796–1801) of her son Paul provides an almost lunatic appendage. Hating his mother, who had sought to bar him from the accession, the new Emperor set himself to undo much of her work. This midget monarch, with his absurd turned-up nose and squeaky voice, was remarkable for the sudden tantrums during which he would summarily consign random victims

ARCTIC
OCEAN

SWEDEN

Stockholm

BALTIC SEA

Helsinki

Archangel

N. Dvina

L. ONEGA

L. LADOGA

Tallin

St Petersburg

Vologda

Novgorod

Vyatka

Perm

Riga

Pskov

Kostroma

Mitau

Tver

Tilsit

L. Dvina

Vladimir

Volga

Ufa

Kovno

Vilna

Borodino

Moscow

Nizhny
Novgorod

Kazan

Grodno

Vitebsk

Kaluga

Smolensk

Warsaw

Minsk

Tula

Penza

Samara

PRUSSIA

Pripet

Mogilyov

Oryol

Tambov

Orenburg

Lublin

Chernigov

Voronezh

Saratov

Austerlitz

Kiev

Kursk

Don

Ural

Buda

Dniester

Poltava

Dniepr

Kharkov

Volga

Tsaritsyn

Pest

AUSTRIA

Jassy

Kishinyov

Yekaterinoslav
Taganrog

Belgrade

Bender

Odessa

Kherson

Azov

Astrakhan

Bucharest

CASPIAN
SEA

Danube

Sevastopol

OTTOMAN

BLACK SEA

EMPIRE

0   450 Mls
0   700 Kms

The Russian Empire at the time of Catherine II (Catherine the Great).

Count Peter Palen (1745–1826), a leading organizer of the Emperor Paul's assassination on the night of 11–12 March 1801. *Right:* The Emperor Paul (reigned 1796–1801).

to Siberia or to a fortress dungeon. But unhinged though many of his policies appear – and not least the proposed conquest of India suddenly ordained at the end of his reign – there were also signs that Paul had the interests of the state at heart, and perhaps more so than his eminent mother, whose autocratic whim had always been supreme. At all events Paul made one statesmanlike contribution when he replaced Peter the Great's unworkable provision of 1722 with a statute basing succession to the throne on the principle of male primogeniture. This was instrumental in protecting the later Romanovs from palace revolutions and dynastic turmoils such as had conferred on the Russian eighteenth century the spirit of a serialized light opera. But the unpopular Emperor's new statute did not save his own life when he was assaulted and strangled on the night of 11–12 March 1801 by a posse of drunken officers fearful of his maniac impulses. Due process of Paul's new law now brought to the throne his eldest son, Alexander I, who had tacitly approved his eccentric father's assassination, having himself been menaced by the imperial caprice.

A view of snow-bound Moscow during the Emperor Paul's reign.

THE EMPIRE IN 1800

To consider the general condition of the Empire on the eve of Alexander I's accession is to be struck by two sharply opposed tendencies. On the one hand there are the giant strides which Russia had made in gaining and consolidating her position as an undisputed major European power. On the other hand there are also the many respects in which this far-flung community still remained economically and culturally backward when compared to the most advanced countries of the West.

From 1724 onwards (this being the date of the first Russian census of male citizens) it becomes possible to chart the rise of the Russian population by means less vague than informed guesswork. In that year the Empire's citizens numbered about fourteen million. Within six decades the total had doubled (to twenty-eight million in 1782–83), and within a further five decades it had more than doubled again: to sixty million in 1835. Though part of a sizeable general increase in European population as a whole, the rate of growth achieved by Russia

97

The Emperor Alexander I (reigned 1801–25). Anonymous portrait. *Right:* Alexander's wife, the Empress Elizabeth. Portrait by Vigée-Lebrun.

was spectacular. For example, Russia almost quadrupled her citizenry within a period (1750–1860) which saw the tripling of the British and the mere doubling of the German population. This Russian expansion did, however, owe much to the annexation of new territory as well as to natural growth.

The Russian population was predominantly rural in 1800, when a little over four per cent of the inhabitants rated as town-dwellers. In a country where each citizen belonged, in law, to a specific social class or estate, the peasantry remained overwhelmingly preponderant so far as mere numbers were concerned. Yet the gentry, a mere one per cent, was by far the most influential estate, embracing practically all individuals with any claim to secular education alongside a fair proportion of gross ignoramuses. The clergy was of comparable size, also numbering about one per cent of the whole. Most of the residue population belonged either to special – and often overlapping – categories, such as those of the military or Cossacks, or were rated as town-dwellers of various kinds, those registered as merchants being the most prosperous. Among these different classes only the gentry was europeanized to any notable extent, though it must be added that this category overlapped with that of the officials who were beginning to dominate an increasingly bureaucratized community. Thus Russia had – and maintained up to 1917, despite progressive erosions – a loose

Building a peasant hut. Etching by J.-B. Le Prince (1768).

The interior of a peasant hut. Print by J.C.G. Giessler (1798).

caste system. The estates were either hereditary in law (gentry and peasantry) or by custom generally followed (clergy and merchants), so that a son usually belonged to the estate of his father. But though social mobility was discouraged, it was by no means ruled out – as the increasing influence of *déclassé* individuals was to show later in the century. It must be added that two of the estates (gentry and clergy) were termed privileged, being exempt from conscription, taxation and corporal punishment – all three inconveniences being, incidentally, administered by the landowning gentry among peasants on their own estates. As for the clergy, though its nominal privileges were far from worthless, the term privileged seems out of place when one considers the lowly status of the average village priest.

Already a multi-national and multi-religious state by 1800, Russia became yet more diverse as the result of further annexations which continued sporadically throughout most of the century. But though these expansions were partly the result of war or military pressure, the wars of the nineteenth century were a relatively distant concern to the Russian heartland, except for the Napoleonic invasion in 1812. No longer battling, as in previous centuries, for her very existence against Turk, Swede and Pole, nineteenth-century Russia could pursue her continued expansion in a relatively detached spirit – and at the expense of these same ancestral foes. Finland was annexed from Sweden in 1809, Bessarabia was taken from Turkey in 1812, and central Poland (including Warsaw) fell to Russia through the Congress of Vienna in 1815. The populations of Poland and Finland could claim a higher level of civilization than their conquerors, and the Russian government accordingly granted both extensive

A St Petersburg merchant and his wife driving in a drozhky.
Eighteenth-century engraving.

Russia's first railway, opened in 1837 to connect St Petersburg with the Emperor's near-by residence at Tsarskoye Selo. Engraving of 1838.

autonomy, only to remove or curtail this privilege in course of time as first the Poles, and eventually the Finns, proved impossible for the imperial administrative system to digest. Among other acquisitions was the Caucasus – including Georgia, Armenia and modern Azerbaydzhan – incorporated piecemeal in a series of irregular gulps which were more or less completed with the surrender of the guerrilla chieftain Shamil in 1859. As a result of these developments the Empire's territory covered 7·8 million square miles by 1855 – compared with 5·7 million at the beginning of Peter the Great's rule.

Continued economic backwardness remained a salient feature of the swelling and pullulating Empire. In particular, the primitive state of communications hampered trade and administration in a realm where such vast distances must be covered. Though an imperial courier, using relays of fresh horses, could cover as many as two hundred miles a day, travelling by sledge over hard snow, a more typical image is that of barges held fast in ice, or of peasant carts bogged down in the impassable mud of spring and autumn. Not until 1830 was the first metalled road constructed between St Petersburg and Moscow, the two cities also being joined by a railway in 1851. But these were only pioneer operations, after which road construction and railway building stagnated –

and despite later spurts were never stepped up to the necessary tempo. So ill was the Empire served with transport that communication between the centre and the Crimean front in 1853–56 was more difficult for Russia, fighting on her own territory, than it was for her distant seaborne western enemies, Great Britain and France. Not until the 1850s did steamer traffic become established to any notable extent on Russian rivers, while the transport of grain and other cargoes was managed in river barges hauled by the muscle power of human teams straining on the banks. In 1800 there had been 600,000 of these barge-haulers working on the Volga and Oka, and in 1851 there were still 150,000 of them.

During the eighteenth century and earlier, conquests in the southern steppes had gradually opened up grain-producing areas of fertile black earth which had remained untilled for centuries owing to the danger from marauding nomads. One result of this expansion was to foster a general division of labour between the black-earth belt of the south, which sent much of its grain to feed the north, and the forested north, where home industries were more extensively cultivated. Another effect was that hemp and flax, previously the leading Russian exports, were overtaken by grain in the 1840s. The chief outlet for grain exports was the rapidly expanding port of Odessa, which became the fourth largest city of the Empire, after St Petersburg, Moscow and Warsaw.

Though industry too lagged behind that of western Europe, the picture was not one of unrelieved backwardness. In 1800 Russia led the world in the production of pig iron, largely as the result of the mining and iron industries founded in the Urals by Peter the Great. In the early nineteenth century, however, metallurgical production stagnated and the manufacture of textiles began to forge ahead.

Considerable backwardness was to be noted in the cultural sphere on the threshold of the nineteenth century. Few indeed, for instance, were the signs that Russia stood poised to astonish the world with her achievements in literature. The eighteenth century had produced no original Russian writing qualified to capture the imagination of the world at large. Indeed, the very literary language had by no means been fully formed, even by 1800, despite the enormous strides made through the experimental but imitative *belles lettres* of the eighteenth century. The advent of Pushkin (1799–1837) and his successors – as poets and, especially, as novelists – was eventually to change this situation until ignorance of Russian literature would seem a deficiency in the intellectual equipment of any educated foreigner. That would have been an incredible prospect for any Russian to contemplate at the time of Alexander I's accession.

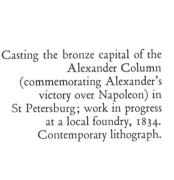

Left: Manuscripts of works by Alexander Pushkin (1799–1837), with cartoons by the poet.

Casting the bronze capital of the Alexander Column (commemorating Alexander's victory over Napoleon) in St Petersburg; work in progress at a local foundry, 1834. Contemporary lithograph.

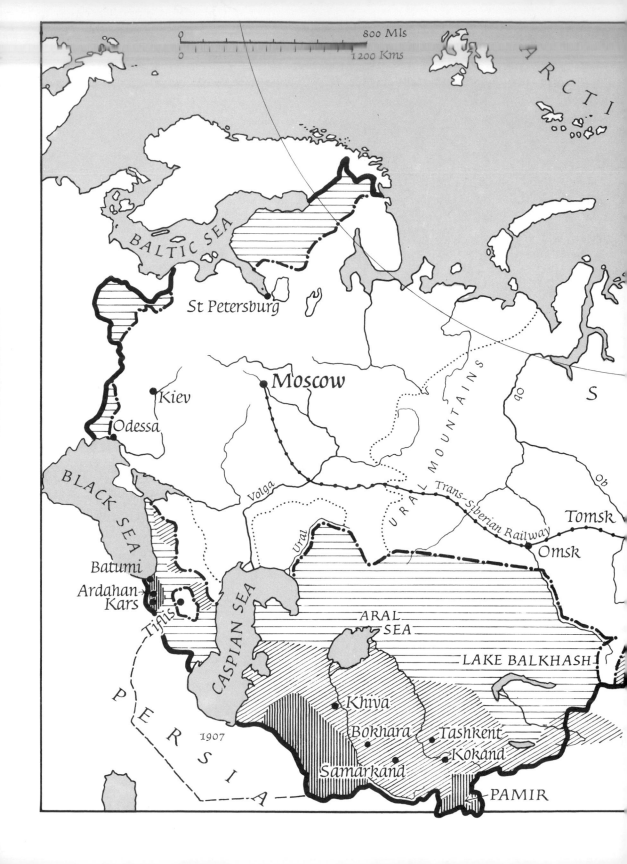

ARCTIC

800 Mls
1200 Kms

BALTIC SEA

St Petersburg

Moscow

Kiev

Odessa

BLACK SEA

Batumi

Ardahan
Kars

Tiflis

Volga

Ural

URAL MOUNTAINS

Trans-Siberian Railway

Ob

Ob

Tomsk

Omsk

S

CASPIAN SEA

ARAL
SEA

LAKE BALKHASH

PERSIA

1907

Khiva

Bokhara

Tashkent

Kokand

Samarkand

PAMIR

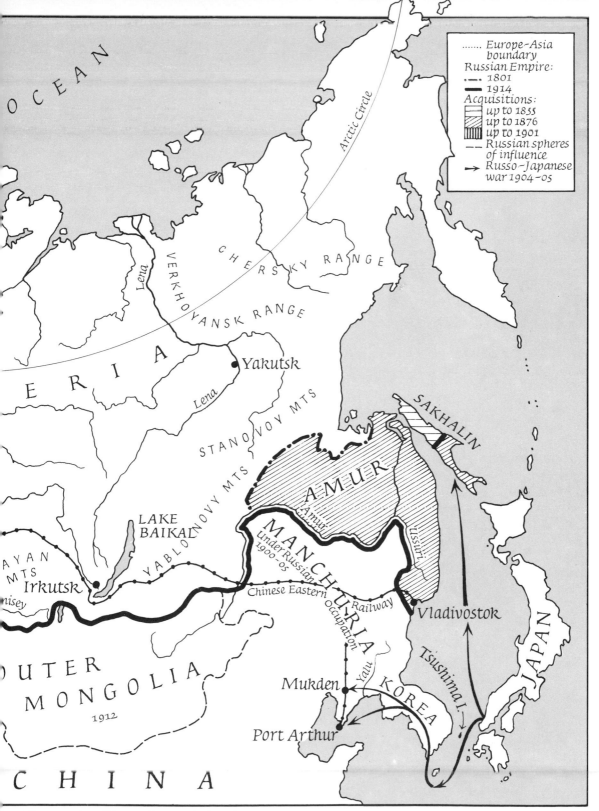

The expansion of the Russian Empire in Asia, 1800–1914.

OCEAN

Arctic Circle

CHERSKY RANGE

VERKHOYANSK RANGE

Lena

Lena

•Yakutsk

STANOVOY MTS

YABLONOVY MTS

LAKE
BAIKAL

AMUR

Amur

SAKHALIN

MANCHURIA

Under Russian
1900-05

AYAN
MTS

Irkutsk

nisey

Chinese Eastern

Occupation

Ussuri

Railway

Vladivostok

JAPAN

OUTER
MONGOLIA

1912

Mukden

Yalu

KOREA

Tsushima I.

Port Arthur

CHINA

ERIA

Significant though Russia's cultural and economic backwardness was, it was her antiquated political and social structure which most seemed to call for overhaul, especially in two features. The first was the autocratic system whereby an individual ruler's sovereign whim could at any moment be translated into law. The second was the continued enslavement of the vast majority of the population, whether as serfs owned by individual masters or as the numerous state peasants whose situation was only slightly less abject.

AUTOCRACY MILITANT

Alexander I (ruled 1801–25) and Nicholas I (ruled 1825–55) were each prepared to recognize, at least in theory, that serfdom should be abolished. Each repeatedly tinkered with the institution, enacting various detailed measures which made little impact on the problem as a whole. One major difficulty for a would-be emancipator was the problem of land ownership. Were serfs to be freed without land? If so they would become destitute, as actually happened to the serfs of the Baltic provinces – liberated but thereby further impoverished under Alexander I. On the other hand, the grant of land to emancipated serfs was also fraught with peril. It was bound to antagonize the owners – members of the gentry, which was the main bulwark of the throne, besides forming the countryside's unofficial police and magistracy. That a hostile gentry could become acutely dangerous neither of these imperial brothers needed reminding, for the assassination by conspiring officers and gentlemen of their father, the Emperor Paul, was not an event which either was ever likely to forget.

While both Alexander I and Nicholas I were agreed on the undesirability of serfdom, they differed – at least in their outward pronouncements – in their attitude to the institution of autocracy. Subtly devious or creatively schizophrenic, Alexander was much given to liberal-minded pronouncements in the style of his grandmother Catherine the Great. Neither Catherine nor Alexander appears to have been a hypocrite, for a glow of sincerity rather than deliberate duplicity was probably uppermost in their minds at the times when they mouthed their high-minded abstractions about equality and brotherly love, while contriving to sponsor the continued enslavement and repression of their subjects. Alexander in particular repeatedly commissioned projects for a Russian constitution, besides actually granting constitutions to the peoples over which he ruled as King of Poland and Grand Prince of Finland. But though constitutional government is generally regarded as incompatible with autocracy, Alexander does not seem to have faced this dilemma. Nor did he, apparently, ever seriously contemplate

View of the palace of 'Mon Plaisir' in the garden at Peterhof (now Petrodvorets), about twenty miles from St Petersburg. Contemporary engraving.

yielding supreme power, being rather concerned to season despotism with benevolent verbiage. As for his younger brother Nicholas, that crowned ramrod was at least open and straight-dealing in his determination to defend the auto-cratic power without equivocation. Another contrast between the two brothers lay in the overriding emphasis given by Alexander to foreign policy. Not that Nicholas was by any means neglectful of Russia's position in the world, but he was chiefly memorable for his effectiveness in regimenting his subjects and setting up effective machinery for suppressing revolutionary urges.

Though it is an error to regard the early years of Alexander I's reign as a period of sweeping liberal reform, certain important changes did take place, especially in the sphere of education and governmental administration. The country as a whole was divided into six huge educational districts, each under its curator.

Michael Speransky (1772–1839), leading
Russian statesman and administrator.

Right: Alexander I and Napoleon confer
on a raft at Tilsit, on the River Niemen, in 1807.

Numerous high schools were founded, while no less than five new universities
(in St Petersburg, Kharkov, Kazan, Derpt and Vilna) joined the original
Russian university of Moscow: all this under a newly established Ministry of
Education. It was at this time, incidentally, that ministries, each under the control of a single individual, were first introduced in place of the collectively managed and outmoded colleges brought in by Peter the Great. The introduction of
ministries helped to streamline administration, but it must also be remembered
that the autocracy tolerated nothing resembling a cabinet system, and that all
ministers were personally appointed – and could be summarily dismissed – by
the Emperor. And though Alexander also set up a State Soviet, or council of
state, in 1810, to scrutinize new legislation, its function was consultative. These
innovations, together with the later codifying of Russian law in 1832, were
largely the work of Michael Speransky, generally considered the most able
administrator in the Empire's history. In a country where extreme competence
has always been suspect (witness the unpopularity of Peter the Great) it is not
surprising that this hard-working and imaginative functionary should have been
disgraced and exiled, as happened in 1812 – though he was eventually to recover
some of his former influence.

In 1805–07, and again in 1812–15, Russia became involved in the gigantic military struggle with Napoleon which included the military defeat of Austerlitz and the great defensive battle of Borodino on Russian soil – the latter closely followed by French occupation of Moscow up to early October 1812. These events, together with the French Grand Army's ignominious flight from the burnt Russian capital, later helped to inspire Tchaikovsky's well-known overture, also contributing many memorable pages to Tolstoy's epic novel *War and Peace*. Russian armies pursued the retreating French, inflicting a series of further defeats and penetrating France itself. Riding into Paris – long regarded by Russians as the cultural centre of the world – on 19 March 1814, the victorious Alexander became the dazzling hero of a pageant more triumphant than any other in the autocracy's history.

The successful punishment of unprovoked aggression by the French greatly boosted Russian patriotism, inspiring a surge of national self-confidence. To that extent the Napoleonic events strengthened the autocracy, fostering a feeling of solidarity between the Russian people and their Emperor. And yet Russian occupation of Europe also had the contrary effect. By bringing so many Russians into direct contact with countries more advanced than their own – countries

which seemed able to function effectively without the blessings of absolute rule and widespread slavery – the campaigns raised awkward aspirations. Russian troops, and particularly their officers, returned home with high hopes of seeing the autocratic system replaced by constitutional government. The common soldiers – conscripted serfs – hoped for demobilization and emancipation.

These expectations were bitterly disappointed when the returning troops found themselves plunged into an orgy of drill parades instead of presiding over the dawn of Russian political freedom. Far from granting his Empire a constitution, Alexander withdrew more and more from the sphere of internal politics in order to play a leading role in the many international conferences which followed the Congress of Vienna. He sponsored the Holy Alliance, whereby the relations between member-states were supposed to be based on Christian principles. He also fell under the sway of various religious fanatics, consigning

The Battle of Borodino, the hard fought engagement of 26 August 1812 which preceded Napoleon's brief occupation of Moscow. Painting by Le Jeune (detail).

the internal administration of his Empire to a vicious and hated reactionary, General Arakcheyev. The Emperor still cultivated benevolently liberal postures, but allowed the realm to sink into reaction and maladministration, his people being crushed by bizarre and repressive measures. Prominent among them was the system of military colonies imposed by Alexander despite opposition even from so harsh an administrator as Arakcheyev. The system involved conscripting peasants as part-time soldiers, while billeting soldiers on them as part-time farm labourers and thus forcing both parties to contribute a double stint. Mutinies occurred in these unpopular institutions, as also in the savagely regimented regular army. They were quelled with the full brutality of Russian military law, which provided for the infliction of up to twelve thousand blows from willow-staves in accordance with the system of passing through the ranks originally ordained by Peter the Great.

Moscow burns as Napoleon's cavalry enters the Kremlin, 2 September 1812. Contemporary engraving.

The five Decembrist leaders who were hanged on a bastion of the Peter and Paul fortress in St Petersburg on 13 July 1826. From Herzen's journal *The Polar Star*, published outside Russia.

Right: The public proclamation of the coronation of Nicholas I (reigned 1825–55) in Moscow. *Below:* Nicholas I returns to the Palace of Facets, in the Moscow Kremlin, after his coronation (1826) in the Uspensky Cathedral, also in the Kremlin. Lithographs by L. Courtin and V. Adam (1828).

Yet during all this time the Emperor remained blind to a threat far more serious than that posed by recalcitrant peasant-soldiers. It was now that educated Russians, chiefly officers, began to form the first conspiratorial movement in Russian history with a claim to be regarded as revolutionary – for it aimed to change the system of government, not merely to unseat an individual ruler. Later known as Decembrists, owing to their unsuccessful coup of December 1825, the plotters hoped to set up a republic, or at least to replace the autocracy with a constitutional monarchy. These activities were on too large a scale to remain entirely secret, especially as Russia already possessed an elaborate though ill co-ordinated network of competing political police organizations. Yet when Decembrist preparations were reported to Alexander he blithely refused to sanction repressive measures, saying that he himself had once shared his disaffected officers' liberal aspirations, and that it was therefore not for him to punish them. That task was assumed with great determination by his successor, Nicholas I, after Alexander had died at Taganrog on 19 November 1825.

The childless Alexander's death sparked off the last dynastic crisis among the Romanovs before the eventual abdication of their last Emperor. Between 27 November 1825, when news of Alexander's decease reached the capital, and

14 December there was an interregnum of seventeen days during which it was not clear whether the throne was to be assumed by Constantine (Alexander's eldest surviving brother) or by Nicholas (the second eldest brother). In fact Constantine had formally renounced his claim several years earlier, but the point is that this renunciation had been kept secret. Troops and officials therefore swore their allegiance to Constantine. Then, when Nicholas's succession was eventually established, the oath of allegiance had to be administered all over again, and to a different monarch – which naturally had an unsettling effect.

The dynasty's embarrassment seemed to present the plotters with their great opportunity. They proceeded, on 14 December, to stage a mutinous demonstration by certain disaffected or gullible St Petersburg garrison troops, who were persuaded by revolutionary officers to parade on the Senate Square in the centre of the capital. Though they were several thousand strong they were ineptly led, making no positive attempt to seize power, while yet refusing to disperse when ordered to do so by the new Emperor. His patience eventually exhausted after repeated attempts to reason with the rebels, Nicholas ordered his artillery to open fire with canister shot and the mutineers fled from the square, leaving many corpses behind. Some tried to cross the River Neva and were drowned when artillery fire smashed the ice around them.

A notorious martinet, Nicholas at once set himself to restore order in his shaken capital, taking an active part in the investigation of the Decembrist conspiracy. Some three thousand persons – civilians and military – were arrested in all. Five of them were judged most culpable and hanged on a bastion of the Peter and Paul Fortress, becoming the first martyrs of the Russian revolutionary movement. Many hundreds of others were exiled to Siberia, while mutinous common soldiers were flogged or transferred to service in the Caucasus.

Determined to forestall any repetition of such indiscipline, Nicholas set himself to quell all revolutionary stirrings among his people. With this in view he set up a unified security police force, consisting of two bodies united under a single commanding officer. The larger was a corps, several thousand strong, of uniformed and mounted gendarmes who were deployed throughout the Empire. The smaller body, the Third Section of His Majesty's Personal Chancellery, consisted of a score or two of officers or civil servants based in the capital. General Alexander Benckendorff, one of the many Baltic Germans who rose high in the imperial service, became the first head of this two-tier political police force. But though Benckendorff rated as the second most powerful individual in the Empire, all real initiative rested with the energetic Emperor, who treated his whole realm as one vast army command. It was his vain ambition to keep all his sixty or seventy million subjects up to the mark by staging sudden inspections, carried out either by himself or by some high-ranking officer. These occasions caused much dismay, but neither they nor Nicholas's habit of appointing army generals to head his ministries was effective in stamping out the gross incompetence and corruption from which his Empire's administration notoriously suffered.

The Emperor's over-all aim of suppressing revolution was, however, achieved. The means were various and included strict control exercised over universities and their syllabuses. Censorship was strengthened, and citizens found their private conversations denounced to the Third Section or to gendarmes by professional spies or enthusiastic amateurs. Thus Russia embarked, for the first time in her modern history, on a systematic campaign of thought control. It was not merely negative, for citizens were also required to subscribe to an official ideology expressed in the triple slogan 'Orthodoxy, autocracy and patriotism'.

These oppressions bore heavily on writers, and since Russian literature first blossomed into true creativity in the 1820s, its initial flowering happened to coincide exactly with a period of acute official repression. No leading author of the period escaped molestation, excepting Gogol, for though such works as his *Dead Souls* and *Inspector General* appeared to mock contemporary society, he was in many ways a supporter of the *status quo*, and even received grants of cash from the Third Section. Among other authors less co-operatively minded, Pushkin was subjected to a prolonged campaign of petty harassment which contributed to the desperate mood in which he met an early death by a duellist's bullet. Herzen, Turgenev, Lermontov and many lesser figures all had their clashes with censorship and police authority. Towards the end of the reign, when oppression became yet more rigorous, Dostoyevsky – still a young and comparatively unknown novelist – was even condemned to death along with twenty others for participating in a political discussion group, the sentence being commuted, and before the very firing squad, to Siberian imprisonment and exile. On the whole, however, the treatment of writers under Nicholas I was ludicrously frustrating rather than downright murderous. There are no parallels whatever in the reign to Stalin's handling of Pilnyak, Babel, Mandelshtam and the many hundreds of lesser writers consigned to Soviet death camps. Nor is the obligation placed by Nicholas I on the publicist Chaadayev – to receive a daily visit from a qualified doctor (the motive being to cast doubts on the sanity of one whose writings were deemed unpatriotic) – comparable in severity to the use of mental institutions as dungeons for the recalcitrant in the Soviet Union of the 1970s.

Alexander Pushkin. Portrait by V. A.
Tropinin.

Nicholas Gogol (1809–52), the author of
Dead Souls. Pencil drawing by Mazer.

The poet and novelist Michael Lermontov
(1814–41). From a lithograph after a
drawing by von Gorbunow.

Alexander Herzen (1812–70), noted
publicist; opponent of the autocratic
system; the most important Russian
nineteenth-century political émigré.
Photograph by Nadar.

The novelist Ivan Turgenev (1818–83).
Painting by Ilya Repin.

The novelist Theodore Dostoyevsky
(1821–81). Lithograph based on a
photograph of 1865.

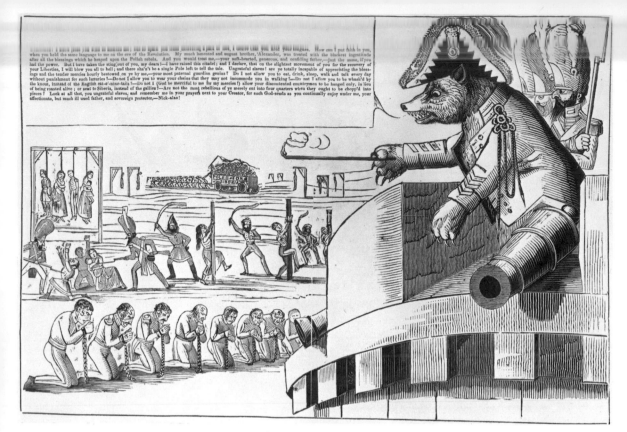

Despite all curbs, Russian literature came of age under Nicholas I as part of a general intellectual ferment. In the 1830s discussion groups, influenced by German idealistic philosophy, flourished, especially in the ambience of Moscow University – at a convenient distance of over 450 miles from the capital dominated by the stern Emperor. The 1840s witnessed the outbreak of impassioned controversy between Westernizers and Slavophils, of whom the former believed that Russia belonged in spirit to Europe and should model her future development on western lines. The Slavophils, by contrast, argued that Russia had her own uniquely valuable culture based on the Orthodox Church and the village commune (a traditional Slavonic institution of much advertised antiquity). Though their views were the less obviously at variance with governmental ideology, the Slavophils too were harassed by officialdom in an age when even praise of the system was suspect, implying as it did that the speaker might have considered himself free to cast blame. The reign also saw the first stirrings of Russian socialism – a Westernizing rather than a Slavophil trend, though some early socialists or near-socialists (notably Herzen) did incorporate Slavophil features in their thinking.

Left: An English cartoon (*c.* 1832), 'The clemency of the Russian monster', shows Nicholas I addressing the Poles after crushing, in 1831, their great rebellion against Imperial Russian rule.

The Emperor Nicholas I (reigned 1825–55). Anonymous painting of 1856 (detail).

Such were the preoccupations, in the age of Nicholas I, of many forerunners of the Russian intelligentsia: a key concept which did not gain currency until the 1870s, when it was first introduced by a minor writer, P. D. Boborykin. Already in the 1830s and 1840s, however, the traits of the future intelligentsia were in evidence: verbosity, excitability, impracticality, high-mindedness and a readiness for quixotic self-sacrifice. To these were added in due course intellectual intolerance, political extremism and no small admixture of sheer dottiness. Whether over-enthusiastic or – as was by no means unknown – comparatively restrained, a member of the intelligentsia was, in any case, by implication one opposed to the Russian government of his day.

The autocratic state was far more brutal in curbing mass insurrections than in quelling intellectual unrest. Horrified by the outbreak of revolution in France and Belgium in 1830, the Emperor found his attention drawn in that same year to a domestic upheaval: the great Polish rebellion, which took a year and a large-scale military campaign to suppress, after which the Poles lost their constitution and most of the autonomy granted to them by Alexander I in 1815. Many Poles were exiled to Siberia. Nearer home, military colonists revolted in the wake of a cholera epidemic in 1831, whereupon the Emperor intervened personally to ordain the mass flogging of the culprits, many of whom perished as a result.

In 1848 a further wave of European revolutions produced a mood of yet blacker reaction in the Autocrat, who sent a large Russian army to the aid of the Habsburg Emperor Franz Josef when his rule was challenged by revolutionary Hungarians. A champion of legitimism everywhere in the world, as was his predecessor, Nicholas earned the nickname 'Gendarme of Europe' by the persistence with which he pursued such policies.

Though the soldier-Tsar made his army feared throughout Europe, his reign ended in a military fiasco which suggested that such alarm had been premature. During the Crimean War of 1853–56 (which arose from Nicholas I's territorial ambitions in south-eastern Europe) British and French forces invaded Russian territory and laid siege to Sevastopol. Ill led and ill organized at the rear, the Emperor's army took a beating on its home territory at the hands of an expedition itself ineptly generalled. Final defeat was delayed until after Nicholas's death, but he perished with the knowledge that his system had failed, and in the very military sphere to which he had always attached supreme importance.

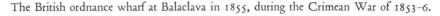

The British ordnance wharf at Balaclava in 1855, during the Crimean War of 1853–6.

Alexander II's accession in 1855 was an event unprecedented in that the new sovereign had been systematically prepared for his imperial destiny to a greater extent than any other Romanov, besides which he also succeeded his father without any accompanying dynastic complications. In keeping with these promising auguries, the new Tsar proceeded to enact sweeping legislation which democratized Russian society in a manner disappointing to political fanatics, whether of the extreme right or left. No other ruler of Russia – Muscovite, Imperial or Soviet – has a comparably benevolent record. Alexander may therefore be contrasted with his greatest reforming predecessor, Peter the Great, who did indeed change Russian society – but in the opposite direction. Where Peter had imposed rigorous controls throughout the community, Alexander considerably loosened them, diminishing – though admittedly to a limited degree – the element of class privilege within the Empire.

The Empire had already grown notably more humane over the years. Such barbarous forms of punishment as quartering, breaking on the wheel, impaling, beheading and the like had already been abandoned in the eighteenth century, and further concessions had been ordained under the first two nineteenth-century Romanovs. Alexander I, for example, declared himself against judicial torture, and abolished the punishment of nostril-slitting. Nicholas I did away with the appalling knout. His son continued this process, curtailing corporal punishment far more drastically, though even after his reforms it could be imposed by peasant courts, in prisons and in army penal units.

The curtailment of flogging was only a minor item in the structure of humane reform sponsored by the Tsar-Liberator. Other relaxations, also relatively minor, had closely followed his accession, and had included the removal of restrictions on foreign travel and the opening of universities to entrants from all social classes, as also the amnestying of the Decembrists and other political prisoners consigned to Siberia under Nicholas I. Such concessions helped to create an atmosphere of relaxation, but were merely the prelude to the series of major reforms introduced by the emancipation of the serfs. This was an event so momentous that the year in which it occurred, 1861, remains the most important single date in nineteenth-century Russian history.

By the middle of the nineteenth century serfdom was widely considered ripe for abolition. It was a blot on Russia's international reputation, it was inhumane, and it was regarded as a prime cause of the inefficiency which had led to the Empire's defeat in the Crimea. It was also dangerous. Perhaps the serfs, who

The Emperor Alexander II
(reigned 1855–81).

were continually staging minor riots, killing landowners and burning manor houses, might one day concert their efforts and mount yet another great peasant revolt along the lines of Pugachov and Razin. Though that prospect was remote in so thoroughly regimented a state, it seems to have been at the back of Alexander II's mind when he declared, in a momentous speech made on 30 March 1856, that 'it is better to abolish serfdom from above than to wait for it to abolish itself from below'.

The emancipation and other enactments of the period present the spectacle of a Tsar, himself no liberal by nature, but a staunch conservative and admirer of his reactionary father, who yet sponsored the most important humane reform in Russian history. He did so against the strong opposition of a vocal section among the serf owners, who feared to lose their property without adequate compensation. But the Tsar did not falter from his declared intention to emancipate, declaring that the serfs must not only be freed, but must also receive land with which to support themselves. How much land? How chosen and how paid for? These key questions caused much argument and discussion. In the end the freed serfs received roughly the area which they had been accustomed to cultivate for their own maintenance. The landlords were compensated by the government, which then exacted redemption payments from the peasantry on an instalment plan spread over forty-nine years.

Alexander II's manifesto of 1861, proclaiming the emancipation of the serfs, is read out in public at Telav, Georgia.

Important though the emancipation was, its nature will be misunderstood if the impression is created, as in some accounts, that the Tsar-Liberator suddenly, by a single stroke of the pen, conferred freedom on an entire homogeneous community of over fifty million peasant slaves. It must be borne in mind that peasant conditions differed widely throughout the country, and that some serfs, in various parts of the Caucasus, were only to be freed several years after 1861, while others (in the Baltic) had already received their liberty under Alexander I. Moreover, the rural community on the eve of emancipation was very far from consisting exclusively, or even in its overwhelming majority, of serfs – that is, of privately owned peasants. Nearly half of the villagers, including the Siberian peasantry as a whole, belonged to the state. Bonded in many ways, but enjoying a status superior to that of the serfs, these were unaffected by the statute of 1861.

123

So too were members of a smaller category, that of the appanage peasants who provided revenue for the imperial household. For both state and appanage peasants separate provision was made.

Such limitations – and others to be mentioned below – on the operation of the Emancipation Statute of 1861 do not alter the fact that it conferred freedom on many millions of men, women and children who had previously been bought and sold like cattle. It remains, therefore, one of the most beneficent pieces of legislation on record. It has also been well noted that Alexander II freed more slaves than Abraham Lincoln – freed them, moreover, several years earlier and without any accompanying civil war. But though the Emperor's achievement was one of momentous moral and symbolic significance, many of its beneficiaries could not see it in that light. Most of the liberated serfs resented receiving too little land for their needs and having to pay far more for it than they could afford. Nor was the freedom granted to them by any means complete, since even after 1861 individual peasants remained bound in various ways to their village communes. These assemblies of village householders took over the administrative functions now lost by the former serf owners: tax collection, the provision of army recruits and the maintenance of order. The commune also became collectively responsible for making the redemption payments. Special community courts received power to order the flogging of recalcitrant peasants, and even to send them to Siberian exile. These powers were similar to those previously enjoyed by individual landlords. The peasantry therefore remained subject to legal discrimination after emancipation. On such grounds the Tsar-Liberator is sometimes described in Soviet historiography as a cunning hypocrite – a despot masquerading as a humane reformer. Kremlin-instructed historians are, by contrast, comparatively kind to Imperial Russia's more authoritarian rulers, such bias against the reforming Tsar perhaps deriving from his temporary effectiveness in diverting Russia from her eventual totalitarian destiny.

Like the emancipation of the serfs, Alexander's other reforms all had the effect of democratizing Russian society to a significant though admittedly limited degree. The legal reforms of 1864 very largely removed the element of class bias from the administration of justice. Independent, irremovable, well-paid judges were appointed, proceedings which would formerly have been held in secret were now held in public, trial by jury was instituted and a Russian bar was established. Based on a close study of foreign models, the legal reforms are generally considered to have been outstandingly effective, though in course of time means were found to lessen their impact.

Alexander II also established a new system of local government to fill the gap left by the termination of the landlords' function as rural administrators. Elective bodies, the zemstvos, were established under an act of 1864. These rural councils became responsible for local education, medical care and road building, being empowered to levy local rates. A similar provision later provided for elective town councils. Yet another blow was struck against traditional privilege with the military reforms of 1874, whereby liability for call-up into the army was extended to the gentry and other categories hitherto immune. Under Nicholas I the period of conscription had been grotesquely long: twenty-five years. It was now reduced to six. Having so large a population, Russia did not require universal conscription, but operated a selective draft from which various categories (for example, only sons) were exempted, besides which educational qualifications were made a basis for reducing the period of compulsory service to as little as six months for university graduates.

To confer widespread benefits is not necessarily to inspire any corresponding degree of gratitude, and it is perhaps not surprising that the reforming Tsar incurred considerable unpopularity – or even that his reign should have ended with his assassination by a revolutionary group. By 1861 the early honeymoon period of the reign was already over. Believing themselves cheated by the terms of the complex emancipation statute, many peasants rioted or waited in vain for a second, real, emancipation, which never came. To the peasants, it was the landlords and officials – rarely the Tsar himself – who became an object of execration. A minority of intellectuals, by contrast, were more inclined to regard the Autocrat as their personal enemy, and to rate him ripe for liquidation as the symbol of a hated and tyrannical system. Such attitudes fostered the rise, in the early 1860s, of the first serious Russian revolutionary movement, whose adherents became known as nihilists – the term applied to them by the novelist Ivan Turgenev in his *Fathers and Children* (1862). Foreshadowing twentieth-century beatniks and hippies with their hirsute appearance, dark glasses and parade of sexual promiscuity, the nihilists likewise threatened to create a new – and yet more solemn – purportedly non-conformist brand of inverted conformity. They championed women's rights, preached utilitarianism in the arts, denounced religion, circulated illegal revolutionary pamphlets, called for the slaughter of the Emperor and finally accomplished it after mounting a campaign of political terror by dagger, pistol and dynamite.

The first attempt on the Tsar's life occurred in 1866, when a twice-expelled student, Dmitry Karakozov, opened fire with a revolver in the Summer Garden in St Petersburg, but missed. In the following year, in Paris, a Pole made an unsuccessful attempt on the sovereign – Alexander had, incidentally, crushed the second Polish rebellion of the century with great ruthlessness in 1863. Personally brave when openly menaced (he once saved a gillie from an enraged bear), the Tsar found it harder to face lurking dangers. He formed the habit of skulking in his palace – a prisoner, almost, of his own police – and allowed his Chief of Gendarmes, Count Peter Shuvalov, to assume the powers of unofficial domestic dictator until his dismissal in 1874. But though several liberal-minded ministers were replaced by diehard reactionaries, Alexander had by no means abandoned the policy of reform even by the end of his harassed reign.

In the 1870s the tiny revolutionary movement expanded until it numbered several hundreds – or thousands – of adherents. A determined attempt was now made to exploit the insurgent potentialities of the peasantry by young political missionaries, chiefly students, who went out into the countryside to enlighten or agitate the villagers. But little effective communication could take place between the canny muzhik and the naïve, more skimpily bearded nihilist youth who sought rustic converts to socialism. The rural invasion failed completely, many of its promoters being arrested. By the end of the decade it had given way to underground urban revolutionary organizations which concentrated increasingly on political terror.

The imperial train is derailed on 19 November 1879 in an unsuccessful attempt to assassinate Alexander II. Contemporary artist's impression.

Michael Loris-Melikov
(1825–88).

The assassination of the Tsar and his leading officials might (it was vainly hoped) induce his terrified successor to embark on more radical reforms. Alternatively, the whole autocratic system might with luck collapse in ruins – to be succeeded by some vaguely conceived utopia. Unrealistic though such aspirations were, they were pursued with utter fanaticism by People's Will, a small group of revolutionary terrorists who assassinated several leading officials, including a chief of gendarmes and a provincial governor, before concentrating their efforts on Alexander's own person. Several abortive attempts were made to mine the imperial train, and a great explosion was engineered under the Emperor's dining-room in the Winter Palace. But for the time being all these efforts were in vain.

As part of his continuing search for means of combating political unrest, Alexander granted domestic dictatorial powers to an energetic and intelligent general, Loris-Melikov, who pursued a dual policy – firmly repressing revolutionary activity on the one hand, but also sponsoring relaxations calculated to remove political grievances. He obtained the Emperor's consent to a scheme empowering members of certain elective bodies to advise the government on legislation – a timid step, but one of some symbolic significance, towards the granting of a constitution such as still remained the focus of liberal hopes. No sooner had the Emperor consented to this proposal in principle, however, than

Scene during the assassination of Alexander II, 1 March 1881. Contemporary artist's impression.

the revolutionaries at last crowned their assassination plans with spectacular success. On 1 March 1881 the Tsar-Liberator was fatally injured by a home-made grenade thrown at him on the Catherine Embankment in St Petersburg. The assassin, who also perished in the explosion, was Ignatius Grinevitsky, one of a four-man bombing squad of People's Will under the tactical command of Sophia Perovsky, a governor's daughter turned terrorist.

The butchered monarch's reign had seen a further vast increase in the Empire's Asiatic territory. In 1858-60, and in the furthest east, the lands north of the Amur, as also the maritime province south of that river's lower basin, were annexed from China through diplomatic pressures. To serve the new annexations the port of Vladivostok was founded (1860). Then, yet further east, Russia obtained the whole of the Island of Sakhalin in 1875. In central Asia, and to the east of the southern Caspian Sea, still larger areas were annexed, or became Russian protectorates. St Petersburg was now the capital of a vast colonial empire, and one unique in that it formed a single territorial block. Not that continued Russian expansion by any means reflected the Emperor's own wishes. Many of his new annexations were the work of colonizing generals on the

The Congress of Berlin, 1878. From a contemporary engraving.

spot who knew that their monarch was too weak to punish them for absorbing vast tracts of Asia contrary to orders issued from the centre – not to mention soothing assurances given to Britain and other European colonial powers. It was also a measure of the Tsar's pliability that he allowed his foreign policy to be influenced by public opinion – a new and rare phenomenon in Russian history – when he accepted the role of liberator of the Balkan Slavs from Turkish rule. The Empire accordingly became embroiled in war against Turkey in 1877–8 – a conflict inspired by the newly arisen Panslavist movement and resulting in the liberation of Bulgaria. In eastern Europe Russia's interests clashed more directly with those of other major powers than was the case in Asia, and she was forced, at the Congress of Berlin (1878), to give up many of the fruits of her victory over the Turks.

The late nineteenth century saw a swing to more reactionary rule during the period bracketed by Alexander III's reign (1881–94) and the first twelve years (1894–1905) of Nicholas II's.

Already nurtured as an extreme conservative by a notoriously diehard tutor (Constantine Pobedonostsev), the bluff, unimaginative, physically tough

'Russian civilization'. An English cartoon of 3 March 1880 showing prisoners travelling under escort to Siberia.

Alexander III was driven even further into that camp through his father's murder by revolutionaries. The constitutional experiment was dropped and its author, Loris-Melikov, resigned, while Pobedonostsev became a potent though vacillating power behind the throne, his official position being that of Chief Procurator of the Holy Synod. Intensified police pressure now threw the whole revolutionary movement on the defensive and crushed terrorism. The demoralized rump of People's Will accordingly abandoned political assassination as a tactic. But though the years 1884–1900 were free from that nuisance, revolutionary opposition continued to smoulder underground and was to flare up with far greater force in the 1900s.

Meanwhile a determined attempt was being made, under the influence of Pobedonostsev and like-minded colleagues, to water down Alexander II's reforms. Though the serfs could not be re-enserfed, they could be – and were – brought back under a measure of gentry control by the introduction of land captains in 1889. These powerful administrator-magistrates helped to erode both Alexander II's emancipation statutes and his judicial reforms. Local government too was conservatized through procedures giving greater power to the gentry. Educational opportunities for the lower classes were also curtailed, and university autonomy was further restricted. Thus Alexander III tried to set back the clock to his grandfather's day, seeking to resurrect ancient privileges and to re-establish 'Orthodoxy, autocracy and patriotism' as the Empire's ideology.

The age was also remarkable for a policy of russification, especially in the alien, western provinces of the Empire, where Baltic Germans and Finns now began to share the earlier destiny of the Poles by joining the ranks of less-favoured subject nations. The Finns were wantonly antagonized, losing many of their rights as a separate nation within the Empire from 1898 onwards. As for the Baltic provinces, Russian replaced German as their official language and the German University of Derpt was russified under the Russian name of Yuryev which the same town (now Tartu) had borne in ancient times. Yet the Emperor himself was of almost pure German descent owing to the policy, initiated by Peter the Great, of marrying potential Russian heirs into German princely families.

As a further aspect of russocentrism, discrimination against the Jews was intensified. The Empire's Jewish population had increased at an even greater rate than that of the country as a whole: from about one million at the end of the eighteenth century to about five million a hundred years later. It was less Judaism, Yiddish speech and alien customs which made the Jews a problem in an empire

The execution of Alexander II's assassins, 1881. Contemporary artist's impression.

which had absorbed many a nationality no less exotic, than the fact that Jews combined these un-Russian characteristics with the lack of any block of national territory. Most of them lived in pockets and ghettos within the Pale of Settlement to which they were legally restricted: certain provinces of the west and south-west roughly coinciding with the area of modern Belorussia and Ukraine. Now, in the late nineteenth century, laxly administered residence restrictions on Jews were tightened up and rigorously enforced, some twenty thousand Jews being brutally evicted from Moscow in 1891. In the early 1880s anti-Jewish riots had broken out, largely inside the Pale, but such outbreaks did not become a major problem until the early 1900s, when the government failed to take effective measures against a new and far worse wave of pogroms. Another hardship imposed on Jews in the late nineteenth century was a quota limiting their entry into high schools and universities. As a result of these and other restrictions over a million Russian Jews emigrated, largely to North America. Among those who chose to stay behind, many joined the swelling revolutionary movement in which Jews had hitherto played only a modest part.

A Jew is beaten, while soldiers fail to intervene, during the Kiev pogrom which followed the assassination of Alexander II. Contemporary artist's impression.

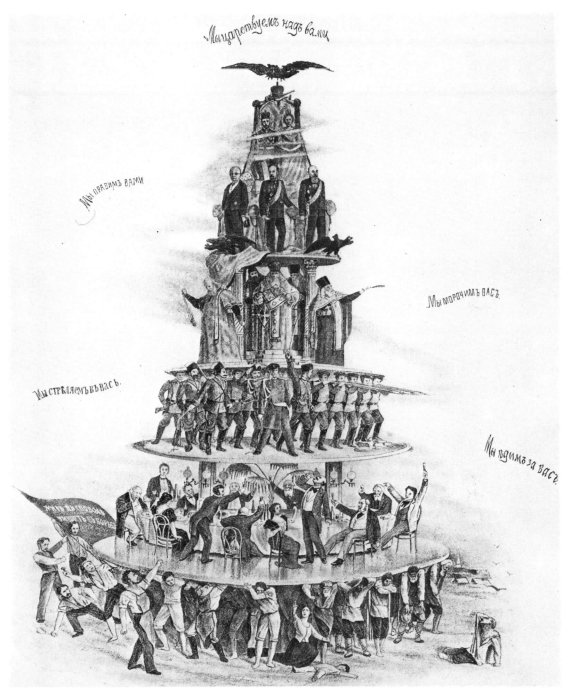

Imperial Russia's social structure derided in an anonymous cartoon of 1900 issued by the Union of Russian Socialists.

The Empire had made enormous strides towards the position of a modern state by the end of the nineteenth century, as becomes especially clear if comparison is made with its backward condition in 1800. And yet Russia's cultural, educational and economic level still remained, in general, considerably lower than that of the leading western European industrial countries. An exception must be made for the arts, and most particularly for prose fiction, in which nine-teenth-century Russian achievements rivalled those of any other country, including as they did the works of Pushkin, Lermontov, Gogol, Turgenev, Tolstoy, Dostoyevsky and Chekhov.

In most other areas generally regarded as indicators of progress Russia's achievements were simultaneously impressive by her own standards and modest by the criteria of the advanced West. For example, Russia entered the twentieth century with a total of nine universities containing some seventeen thousand students, whereas the year 1800 had found her with Moscow University alone – and even in 1809, after the foundation of two additional universities, the number of students had been a mere 450. By 1900, moreover, Russian students had established a tradition of political protest which – from the viewpoint of the early 1970s – might seem to put them in the very van of modernity. And yet the proportion of illiterates in the Empire's population at large was enormous, being recorded (in 1897) at seventy-four per cent of persons between nine and forty-nine.

As such statistics indicate, Russia was still very largely a nation of benighted muzhiks and still remained a predominantly rural society. But urbanization too had made great advances in the nineteenth century, for thirteen per cent of the population rated as urban in 1897, by contrast with the mere four per cent of a century earlier. As for the Empire's overall population, the census of 1897 – the only systematic general census to be conducted in the Imperial period – showed a total citizenry of over 128,000,000: an increase of three and a half times in the century. Industrialization had also progressed apace, a labour force of some three million having been built up by 1900. At less than three per cent of the popula-tion this was, again, a small figure by comparison with that of British or German workers, but represented a fifteenfold increase over the very approximate figure of 200,000 industrial workers within the Empire a hundred years earlier.

Though the emancipation of the serfs had not stimulated the immediate boost to the economy predicted by some optimists, Russia's industrial revolution did occur in due course, beginning in the late 1880s. During the 1890s, the great period of Russian economic take-off, the growth rate for industrial output

The novelist Leo Tolstoy (1828–1910).

The short-story writer and dramatist Anton Chekhov (1860–1904) with his wife, the actress Olga Knipper.

The writer Maxim Gorky (1868–1936), centre, with the theatrical producer Constantine Stanislavsky and the actress Mary Lilin.

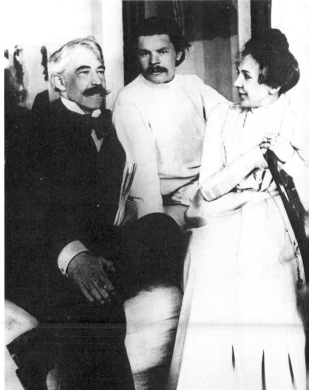

Alexander Borodin (1833–87).

Modest Musorgsky (1839–81).

Nicholas Rimsky-Korsakov (1844–1

Four Russian composers of
the late nineteenth century.

Peter Tchaikovsky (1840–93) with two of the
singers who took part in the first performance
of his opera *The Queen of Spades* (1890).

averaged about eight per cent per annum. This spurt was followed by a lull in the years 1900–07, after which the economy took off again at a slightly more modest rate (between six and seven per cent) during the seven years preceding the First World War.

Important nineteenth-century economic advances included the development of iron-works and coal-mining in southern European Russia to the point where the Donets Basin overtook Peter the Great's original industrial base in the Urals. Caucasian oil production soared until Russia was producing more oil than the rest of the world put together during the four-year period 1898–1901. The Russian railways were also very considerably expanded, one especially important landmark being the construction of the great Trans-Siberian line from 1891 onwards. Siberia was now increasingly opened up, and the state helped – most systematically from 1905 onwards – to organize the transport of peasant settlers to these fecund virgin vastnesses, thus alleviating the chronic land hunger which always seems surprising in so huge a country. To these developments must be added the growth of banking and joint-stock companies, the stabilization of Russian finances and the success with which Russian industrial enterprises began to attract foreign and eventually native finance.

A hundred-rouble note, issued in 1898, depicting Catherine the Great.

Russian peasant immigrants in Siberia and (*below*) convicts working in the mines. Late nineteenth-century engravings.

The Emperor Alexander III (reigned
1881–94) with his family.

All these features of a thrusting civilization and economy contrasted vividly
with the antique traditions of the Russian court, and with the autocratic system
which still maintained the trappings of oriental despotism in a world of oil
derricks, steamships and railway trains. As for the late nineteenth-century
emperors, the gigantic Alexander III at least had the presence of a despot,
whereas his dapper, courteous little son, Nicholas II, seemed ill fitted for absolute
command over 120,000,000 subjects. Yet Nicholas too was stubborn in his
attempted defence of autocratic power. A pupil of Pobedonostsev, like his
father before him, he believed that it was God's will for him to preserve the autocracy intact – an assumption in which he was to prove fatally mistaken.

Nicholas's accession in 1894 coincided with a growing ground-swell of
conspiratorial revolutionary activity. In 1898 the first Marxist party was formed
under the title of the Russian Social Democratic Labour Party. In 1903 it split
into the two opposed factions of Mensheviks and Bolsheviks, and it was the
latter wing – the more conspiratorial and the tougher in its methods – which was
to seize power in October 1917 under Lenin's leadership, eventually developing

Left: A cartoon celebrating the assassination on 15 July 1904 of V.K. Pleve, Minister of the Interior and notorious as an oppressor of minority peoples within the Empire. *Right:* Front page of the revolutionary weekly *Zritel* ('Observer'), published in St Petersburg in 1905.

into the present-day Communist Party of the Soviet Union. In the early twentieth century, however, the Social Democrats – who placed their main political hopes in the comparatively small urban working class – seemed less of a menace to the state than the rival Socialist Revolutionaries. As heirs of the Populists who had participated in the missions to the countryside of the 1870s, these looked to the revolutionary potentialities of the peasant masses scouted as politically imbecile by the Social Democrats. The Socialist Revolutionaries also revived, but on a greatly increased scale, the policy of political assassination once pursued by People's Will. After the murder of the Minister of Education, Bogolepov, by a student in 1901, political killings gradually gathered momentum, two Ministers of the Interior (Sipyagin and Pleve) being among the early victims. To counter such assaults the police made widespread use of *agents provocateurs* masquerading as revolutionaries. Since revolutionary agents were simultaneously engaged in penetrating the police, a situation of some complexity arose – so much so that a highly paid spy, Yevno Azef, was able to function as head of the Socialist Revolutionary Party's main murder squad for several years

Cartoon on a postcard of the Russo-Japanese War period showing the 'protective' Russian attitude towards Korean victims of the Japanese.

before his police affiliations were unmasked. Azef was only the most prominent among numerous double, triple, quadruple or even more multiple agents who were often confused as to their own ultimate allegiance. Such an atmosphere, in which the forces of law and order were inextricably mixed up with currents of lawlessness and disorder, helped to breed general demoralization, thus paving the way for the revolutions of 1905 and 1917.

It may perhaps seem surprising that parties dedicated to the overthrow of the state, such as the Social Democrats and the Socialist Revolutionaries, should have been able to maintain a certain amount of legally permitted activity alongside their underground plottings, but this was nevertheless the case. Nor was opposition to the state by any means confined to apostles of violent upheaval. It was, rather, a common attitude among the majority of educated people, who included – even in Russia – a substantial proportion of moderates. Tending at times to lump such moderates together with revolutionary fanatics, and to treat both as equally pernicious, the authorities made a tactical error which could only help the forces of extremism.

Russians in the Moscow fruit market, during September 1905, read about the achievement of peace with Japan and the plan to establish a Russian State Duma.

DECLINE AND FALL

Russian territorial expansion had virtually ceased in the early 1880s, Alexander III having accomplished the feat – unique among the Tsars – of preserving peace throughout his reign, a few minor skirmishes in Central Asia excepted. Nicholas II did not maintain this happy record, allowing himself to be drawn by empire-building advisers into a war (1904–05) with Japan for control over Korea. Another emergent industrial nation, Japan proved the stronger of the two, inflicting crushing naval and military defeats on the cumbrous and logistically extended Empire in the far east.

This unpopular war, waged by an increasingly unpopular Emperor, had unhappy domestic repercussions too, for it helped to bring on the first real, though unsuccessful, Russian revolution in 1905. The upheaval was provoked by a tragic error committed when the Tsar's advisers ordered troops to open fire on peaceful processions of unarmed workers as they approached the Winter Palace in St Petersburg under the leadership of the priestly trade-union leader Father George Gapon. Occurring on Sunday 9 January 1905, the episode caused hundreds of fatalities and introduced the phrases Bloody Sunday and Bloody Nicholas into Russian vocabulary.

Cossack troops at the Baku oil-wells during the revolutionary year 1905.

Workers outside the Putilov iron and steel works in St Petersburg in early January 1905.

A procession in Warsaw in response to the Emperor's manifesto of 17 October 1905, which promised extensive civil rights within the Russian Empire, thereby reviving Polish hopes of national independence. The White Eagle (the Polish national emblem) is displayed.

The 1905 Revolution did not involve any concerted attempt by oppositionist groups to seize power. Rather was it a general collapse of authority accompanied by sporadic, scattered outbreaks of violence, as also by strikes – of professional people as well as of workers – culminating in a general stoppage throughout the Empire. There were widespread peasant riots and there were mutinies within the armed forces, among which the seizure of the battleship *Potemkin* by its insurgent crew has captured the imagination of posterity. Nor was the revolution an exclusively Russian affair, for subject peoples on the periphery of the Empire – Balts, Poles, Caucasians – also attempted to lay violent claim to their rights.

One important symbolic event of the revolutionary year was the establishment of the St Petersburg Soviet. 'Soviet' is simply the ordinary Russian word for 'council', so that the name carried no inflammatory political implications at the time – how could it when one of the most august bodies in the realm, founded by Alexander I in 1810, was called the State Soviet? But as a symbol of workers' power, dominated by the dynamic young revolutionary orator Trotsky, the St Petersburg Soviet attracted considerable attention before the police arrested its members *en masse* on 3 December 1905. This episode was followed by an insurrection in Moscow which was savagely crushed by regular army units, including artillery.

The 1905 Revolution was put down by military force, and the Emperor was firmly in the saddle again by the following year. But though he still retained the title of Autocrat, he was, strictly speaking, an autocrat no more. As a concession to political opposition he had permitted the formation of an elective body, the State Duma: a parliament in embryo. The Duma was undemocratically elected by a franchise weighted in favour of groups deemed loyalist, besides which its decisions were subject to veto by a partly appointive upper house (the State Soviet), and also by the Tsar himself. But since new legislation could not – at least in theory – be enacted without the Duma's consent, a crack had at last appeared in the façade of absolute power.

Four Dumas were elected in all, of which only the third (1907–12) ran its full course of five years, the first and second having been prematurely dissolved by the Emperor in 1906 and 1907, while the fourth lapsed as a result of the Revolution of February 1917. The Duma's powers, never very great, were progressively eroded by the sovereign. Nevertheless, in Russian conditions, the

The Emperor opens the first session of the First State Duma in the Winter Palace, St Petersburg, 27 April 1906.

institution did seem to hold out some prospect of democratic evolution, though many were disposed to condemn it as a mere talking shop. But over-volubility was all too natural a phenomenon in a country so long gagged by political censorship, from which speeches in the Duma were exempted. General censorship of the printed word was also very largely abandoned after 1905.

The 1905 Revolution was followed by a reaction against violence and chaos as the Empire resumed its economic progress. One feature of the period was an attack on illiteracy, part of a development of elementary education involving a fifty per cent increase in the number of primary schools between 1908 and 1913. Considerable efforts were also made to improve the lot of the peasantry. Loans from the newly expanded State Land Bank for the Peasants enabled the more enterprising villagers to increase their holdings, and the state-sponsored settlement of Siberia was further extended. An attack was also made on the institution

A student agitator harangues a group of peasants during the 1905 Revolution. Contemporary artist's impression.

Two cartoons of late 1905 ridiculing the Emperor's famous manifesto of 17 October, which promised freedom of assembly (derided, *left*) and – in effect – a constitution (compared to a house of cards, *right*).

of the village commune by new legislation enabling individual villagers to opt out of that archaic institution. Instead of farming on strips which were periodically re-allotted by their commune, those who wished could now consolidate their land in a single farm which became the individual farmer's personal property. Before the monarchy fell about a quarter of the peasants had seized this opportunity to become individual yeomen – a conservative bulwark of the *status quo*, it was vainly hoped.

This important agrarian reform was the work of Peter Stolypin, who held the joint posts of Minister of the Interior and Prime Minister between 1906 and 1911. 'Prime minister' is, however, a misleading term for the mere chairman of a Soviet of Ministers who continued to be appointed and dismissed by the Emperor, and who remained individually responsible to him alone. Even so Stolypin proved to be one of those Russian statesmen – such as the earlier Loris-Melikov – who might well have achieved considerably more had their careers not been suddenly cut short, in Stolypin's case by an assassin's bullet at a gala performance in the Kiev opera house on 1 September 1911. The murderer was one of those shadowy figures – half police agent, half revolutionary terrorist – whose ultimate allegiance remains a mystery.

In August 1914 the Russian Empire became drawn into the First World War, on the side of the Allies and against the Central Powers, as the result of championing Serbian independence when this was menaced by Austria-Hungary. Though at first welcomed with patriotic enthusiasm by the Russian population as a whole, the conflict was unhappily timed, since it broke out during a period when the Empire's peaceful evolution into a modern democratic state seemed at least a possibility. Any such chance was doomed by disasters on the fronts, beginning with the rout of the Russian Second Army at Tannenberg in the first weeks of the war. The ensuing campaigns were remarkable for the courage shown by the ordinary Russian soldier, but also for the gross deficiencies of an economy which proved unable to supply him with boots, rifles and ammunition in adequate quantity. At home the war led to a bitter political conflict between the Emperor, court and ministers on the one hand, and 'society' on the other – that is, numerous zemstvo members, industrialists, Duma delegates and professional persons in general. Such people were eager to contribute to the successful prosecution of the war, and felt bitterly frustrated when cold-shouldered by the Emperor and his closest advisers.

President Poincaré of France and the Emperor Nicholas II on the yacht *Standard*, July 1914.

The Emperor Nicholas II (reigned 1894–1917) with his family.

Dissatisfaction changed to despair after the Emperor had personally assumed supreme command of the armed forces in August 1915. During his prolonged absences at GHQ the appointment of ministers came increasingly under the control of the Empress Alexandra. Stubborn and unpopular, she had herself fallen under the influence of the notorious bogyman Rasputin, a Siberian peasant reputedly able to allay by hypnotic means the otherwise incurable bleeding to which the haemophiliac Crown Prince Alexis was subject. This medico-political partnership between exalted Empress and demon-seer was a demoraliz-ing spectacle for an embattled nation to contemplate, and the rumour spread that Rasputin and Alexandra – herself of German origin, like almost all the Russian Emperors' wives – were engaged in betraying the Empire to the Kaiser. Though the rumour was unfounded, as was also the gossip claiming that Alexandra and Rasputin were lovers, it was widely believed and led to a general feeling of helplessness. Nor was the practice of appointing and dismissing ministers in rapid succession calculated to restore morale, especially as some of them seemed barely sane. Finally, three ultra-conservative conspirators assassi-nated Rasputin in December 1916, hoping to save the monarchy. By now, however, the rot had gone too far.

A street scene during the period of Russian mobilization in 1914.

When, in February 1917, the end came, it arrived almost casually. Power was not seized by any revolutionary party, but simply collapsed. The immediate cause was a local shortage of bread in Petrograd (as St Petersburg had been renamed in 1914), which led to riots on the streets such as had occurred previously. On this occasion, however, the Cossacks and troops garrisoned in the capital eventually sided with the rioters after a few days of growing confusion, thus producing a situation in which Nicholas was persuaded to abdicate. He was more inclined to do so as the result of advice from most of his main commanders in the field urging or implying that he should lay down his power.

Thus, on the evening of 2 March 1917, the last Tsar-Emperor gave up his throne after the Empire had lasted for nearly two centuries and the Romanov dynasty for more than three.

Chapter Four

PROVISIONAL GOVERNMENT

For nearly eight months of 1917 (3 March to 25 October) Russia was ruled by a Provisional Government consisting at first mainly of leading liberals from the State Duma (which itself ceased to function), and later of coalitions including more socialists alongside liberals. The first Prime Minister was Prince George Lvov, who was followed by Alexander Kerensky from July onwards. But successive cabinet reshuffles could not conceal the fact that this was an admini-stration precarious and ineffectual in the extreme. Lacking any proper legal basis, the new government was never conceived as more than a caretaking body entrusted with power only until such time as a Constituent Assembly could be elected by the people as a whole.

From the beginning considerably more potential influence was wielded by a rival power centre: the Petrograd Soviet of Workers' and Soldi ' Deputies, which had been created on the model of the 1905 St Petersburg Soviet d was vaguely supported by a nation-wide organization of regional Soviets. It was to the Soviets, and not to the Provisional Government, that the Petrograd garrison (already the decisive force in mounting one revolution) owed its allegiance, and the Soviets might consequently have seized power from the Provisional Government at any moment – had they not been deterred from doing so by revolutionary dogma. The Mensheviks (the dominant faction within the early 1917 Soviets) had been taught that the proletarian revolution, towards which they were ultimately working, must be preceded by a period of 'bourgeois' rule. Bourgeois rule of a sort having been provisionally established, the Mensheviks must tolerate it until history should again erupt – a policy in which the other dominant faction in the Soviets, that of the less dogma-ridden Socialist Revolu-tionaries, was prepared to co-operate. With opponents such as these it is hardly surprising that the Bolsheviks should have triumphed in the end. They too were represented in the Soviets, but at first as a comparatively small party. They also

Mutinous soldiers carry a revolutionary banner inscribed 'Liberty, Equality, Fraternity' in the Petrograd streets during the February Revolution of 1917.

lacked effective leadership – but only until Lenin arrived at Petrograd's Finland Station on 3 April, having been permitted by the Kaiser's government to make part of his journey from Switzerland by sealed train through Germany.

Unquestionably the greatest revolutionary in history, Lenin had emigrated from the Russian Empire in 1900 in order to work for the overthrow of the Tsar's government from various countries of western and central Europe, where he was comparatively free from molestation by the Russian police. During the war years Switzerland had been the base from which he sought – through propaganda and international anti-war conferences of socialists – to convert the struggle between nations into a world-wide struggle between classes, working for the defeat of his own country in the belief that he was advancing the cause of revolution. The return of this political firebrand to his native Russia was also an indirect blow against Russia's allies in the west.

Since the eastern fronts were now comparatively inactive, and since Petrograd itself remained the scene of sporadic violence, it is all too easy to forget that a state of war continued to exist between Russia and Germany throughout the revolutionary year. As for the German decision to permit Lenin to proceed to Petrograd by way of German territory, it was an act of war, and a most successful device at that, for it was eventually instrumental in knocking Russia out of the conflict altogether, thus freeing the Central Powers to concentrate on the west. Not that Lenin was a foreign agent – as was commonly suggested at the time – since his determination to exploit Germans, or anyone else, far exceeded their determination to exploit him. Having arrived on Russian soil, he at once ran true to German hopes by demanding an end to hostilities, and by de-nouncing those among his fellow-Bolsheviks who had been supporting the Russian war effort. Lenin also urged the Soviets to take power, even though they were still dominated by his socialist rivals: the Mensheviks and Socialist Revolutionaries. Thus, from the moment of his triumphal entry into Petrograd, Lenin created an impression which was to contribute much to his eventual victory: that of being one man, among many bewildered millions, who completely knew his own mind.

Lenin's revolutionary strategy was deployed against a background of riotous upheaval in keeping with many indications from earlier history that the Russian as a political animal is unhappy at any intermediate point between total regimen-tation and total anarchy. The February Revolution had above all been a general

Petrograd, 29 August 1917. Sailors arriving in the city in order to fight against Kornilov.

Alexander Kerensky, Prime Minister
of Russia July–October 1917.
A photograph taken
at the time of his downfall.

overthrow of authority – on the fronts where the uniformed peasants took to
lynching their officers and to deserting in droves, in the countryside where local
rustics combined with these same deserters to seize the landowners' estates, and
above all in a capital city increasingly given over to mobs and turmoil. On 3–4
July particularly appalling riots occurred as sailors and soldiers, and also
armed workers, rampaged through Petrograd looting and shooting. Though the
Bolsheviks made some attempt to calm the inflamed mob, the impression
nevertheless arose that they, as the most militant of the socialist parties, had
attempted to stage a *coup d'état*. It turned out, however, that the Provisional
Government still possessed sufficient authority to quell the riots, and also to take
measures against the Bolsheviks and their supporters, some of whom (including
Trotsky) were arrested, while others (including Lenin) went into hiding. For
the time being comparative order had been restored.

Kerensky now became Prime Minister – a socialist who believed in pro-
secuting the war against Germany, while attempting to hold domestic disintegration at bay, his main weapon in both campaigns being an impassioned
style of oratory. He suffered the typical fate of the humane, well-intentioned
leader who urges compromise in an age of violence: increasing unpopularity
with all political factions. In August, General Lavr Kornilov, the army commander-in-chief whom Kerensky himself had appointed, decided to mount a
coup d'état with the aim of re-establishing military and social discipline. But
when Kornilov attempted to send his troops against Petrograd, unco-operative
railway workers and political agitators were effective in preventing the army

from moving.

Kornilov's failure helped to strengthen the Bolsheviks, who swiftly recovered, gaining more support among the Petrograd garrison troops as well as building up their own organization of armed workers. In September they obtained a majority in the Petrograd and Moscow Soviets, and on 25 October they seized power in the capital by armed *coup d'état* in the name of the Soviets now dominated by them. Their main strategist remained Lenin, who had long been urging direct action on comrades more reluctant, but who remained in hiding until the last moment, while the detailed tactics of the operation were largely Trotsky's work. The chief event was the seizure of the Winter Palace and of the Provisional Government's ministers, who were conferring there while their leader Kerensky was vainly attempting to drum up support outside Petrograd among troops less disaffected than those of the city garrison.

Most of the rest of the country, including all its central areas, fell to the Bolsheviks without a struggle, local centres being merely informed of the revolution by telegram. The takeover was not entirely bloodless, however, for it was only after a week of hard fighting that Moscow fell to Bolshevism.

The Winter Palace, Petrograd, 1917.

Lenin and Jacob Sverdlov (Chairman of the All-Russian Central Executive Committee) inspect a monument to Marx and Engels in Moscow, 7 November 1918.

RUSSIA UNDER LENIN

By contrast with the February upheaval – a mere collapse of power – the Bolshevik Revolution of October 1917 was a positive seizure of control by armed *coup d'état*. For such an act the Party had been fitted by Lenin's long-standing insistence on rigorous discipline. But could an organization of two to three hundred thousand Bolsheviks – not yet notably well disciplined to the eye of the casual observer – maintain permanent control over a community of so many millions? Much as their popularity had increased during late 1917, Lenin's followers did not enjoy majority support, for the largely rustic nation favoured the Socialist Revolutionaries. The precariousness of the new rulers' position was further emphasized by the contrast between their Marxist revolution – occurring in backward, under-industrialized Russia – and Karl Marx's claim that proletarian revolution would first strike the advanced capitalist countries of the West. Conscious of this contradiction and of their own weak position, the ruling Leninists pinned their hopes for survival on a chain reaction of successful new revolutions, which (they believed) would be sparked off in Germany and elsewhere by the Russian October uprising. This waning hope helped to sustain the Bolsheviks for some years.

Meanwhile Lenin had set himself from the beginning to strengthen his tenuous hold on Russia by energetic gestures and legislation. Immediately on seizing power he promulgated two decrees designed to enhance Bolshevik popularity. In one he called for an end to the war. By the other he nationalized land, but in terms suggesting that the peasants would retain possession of their holdings (which Stalin was to collectivize a dozen years later). When Socialist Revolutionaries complained that Lenin had coolly appropriated their own agrarian programme, he was not greatly perturbed, especially as the Socialist Revolutionaries had now split into two opposing groups, Right and Left. The latter supported the Bolsheviks, which enabled Lenin to create the temporary illusion of a multi-party coalition.

That Lenin intended to outlaw all parties other than his own became evident when the long-awaited Constituent Assembly met on 5–6 January 1918. The Bolsheviks had not been able to prevent the formation of this body through the only free election in Russian history, held in the preceding November. Though the election gave the Bolsheviks only 168 deputies out of a total of 703, which included 380 Right and 39 Left Socialist Revolutionaries, Lenin was able to have the Assembly dispersed by armed force, so that its first meeting also became its last. Russia's sole essay in government by genuine popular representation had thus begun and ended within a span of twenty-four hours.

Lenin's cabinet, the Soviet of People's Commissars, prompted much new legislation. The calendar was reformed, old-style 31 January 1918 being followed immediately by 14 February, which brought Russia into line with western Europe. On 11 March the seat of government was transferred to Moscow after a period of 206 years during which St Petersburg/Petrograd had been the capital. Another change of name occurred when the official designation of Russia was altered to RSFSR (Russian Soviet Federative Socialist Republic). Not until four years later, in 1922, was the name USSR (Union of Soviet Socialist Republics, or Soviet Union) also adopted, to mark the amalgamation of the giant RSFSR with the Belorussian, Ukrainian and Transcaucasian Republics. Since then the total of Union Republics has risen to fifteen. The ruling party, too, sustained a change of name in 1918, when it became the Russian Communist Party (of Bolsheviks). The original title, Russian Social Democratic Labour Party (which had embraced both Bolsheviks and Mensheviks), was thus abandoned by Lenin's followers. In 1922 'All-Union' was substituted for 'Russian'.

Since the new Soviet government lacked any regular military establishment, Trotsky proceeded to build up a new force, the Red Army, on his appointment as People's Commissar (i.e. Minister) for War in early 1918. But though Communist Party members joined up and helped to stiffen morale, they were still few in number and lacked military experience, for which reason Trotsky drafted ex-officers of the former régime into the Red Army. He forced them to serve by means of threats to their families, and appointed political commissars to supervise their activities.

On 3 March 1918 a Bolshevik delegation signed the peace treaty of Brest-Litovsk with Germany. Lenin personally insisted on this agreement in order to give his new government a breathing-space. How hard he had to argue against his colleagues – for he was by no means an absolute dictator ruling by fiat –

Workers, enrolled in the Red Army, undergo rifle training, 1918.

Leo Trotsky (1879–1940) addresses Red Army soldiers in Moscow.

Trotsky (second from left) and Kamenev (right) leaving Brest-Litovsk during the peace negotiations of 1918.

may be judged from the humiliating terms. Through the treaty itself and other developments of the period Russia lost 62,000,000 citizens and 1,300,000 square miles of territory painstakingly annexed by the Tsars over the preceding three centuries. Among the losses were Finland, Estonia, Latvia, Lithuania, Poland, the Ukraine and much of Belorussia. Russia also lost three-quarters of her iron and coal mines, a third of her factories and vital sources of grain.

A further stage in the establishment of one-party control was reached on 6 July 1918, when the Left Socialist Revolutionaries staged an inept *coup d'état* which was promptly suppressed. Though it was not until 1921 that they, and other left-wing undesirables, were finally eliminated from Soviet politics, neither they nor any of the other non-communist socialist parties played any significant role after 1918, while parties further to the right – such as the liberal Kadets – had been proscribed almost from the outset. Nor were the former Emperor and Empress spared. Together with their five children and certain servants they were riddled with bullets and bayoneted in the cellar of their last prison, in Yekaterinburg, at midnight on 16–17 July 1918.

According to Trotsky the murder was ordered by Lenin with the object of denying a possible rallying-point to the opponents of the new Soviet government. Known collectively as 'Whites', these consisted of formerly privileged persons, politicians of rightist or left-wing non-communist persuasion, and sections among the minority peoples. On 30 August 1918 anti-Bolshevik sentiment received violent expression when the Petrograd political police chief,

Uritsky, was assassinated and an attempt was made on the life of Lenin. These two events (which occurred independently, though each was the work of a Socialist Revolutionary) were followed by brutal reprisals. In Petrograd over five hundred hostages, largely members of the pre-revolutionary privileged classes, were shot, as announced by the newspaper *Izvestiya* on 3 September 1918. The massive reprisals in Petrograd and elsewhere marked an intensification of the openly proclaimed campaign of Red Terror administered by the Cheka (the first Soviet political police force). That Lenin meant to rule by methods more violent than those of any nineteenth-century Tsar was now clear, and the Cheka eventually executed or imprisoned victims by their tens of thousands. The Red Terror was officially defended as a response to the anti-Bolshevik atrocities committed by the White forces with which Lenin's Russia was now locked in combat.

The Civil War of 1918–21 was an additional ordeal for a nation already racked by world war and revolution. It was a struggle for the survival of Bolshevism fought by the Reds – who held Moscow, Petrograd and the Great Russian heartland – against the Whites, who were united in a wish to overthrow the Soviet government but had little else in common. The bulk of the forces on both sides consisted of ideologically apathetic peasants impressed at gun point, the country also being ravaged by politically unattached marauding gangs which seemed to have sprung fully armed out of the Time of Troubles.

As a potential asset (at least for a few months) in the continuing war against Germany, the Whites received sporadic military support from the Allied powers. This began at a time when Britain, France and the United States were still at war with the Germans, who (it was feared) might now seize certain huge dumps of military stores previously bestowed on Russia by these same members of the alliance from which Lenin had suddenly and inconveniently withdrawn. The British and Americans established small forces in the Murmansk and Archangel areas of northern Russia to safeguard the military material there stockpiled. Intervention also took place in the south of European Russia, in parts of central Asia and (with considerable Japanese participation) in Siberia. With the defeat of the Central Powers, in November 1918, Allied intervention in Russia assumed the aspect of a half-hearted anti-Bolshevik crusade – so half-hearted that it may even have assisted the Reds, helping as it did to rally Russians in a common dislike of alien intruders.

The Whites attacked the Soviet heartland in various areas on its vast periphery, the eastern and southern fronts presenting the greatest danger to Moscow.

The British intervention. General Lord Rawlinson interrogates a Bolshevik prisoner in northern Russia, September 1919.

In the east the Whites penetrated as far as Kazan and Simbirsk. The White leader, Admiral Kolchak, became nominal commander-in-chief over all their forces, with his headquarters at Omsk in Siberia, being also generally recognized by the anti-Bolshevik organizations as the supreme ruler of Russia. His armies were unable to link up with other theatres, however.

The menace from the south was also serious, coming from the Volunteer Army under General Denikin, which swept forward as far as Oryol, 250 miles from Moscow, in the autumn of 1919. Petrograd was endangered in the same year by General Yudenich until Trotsky arrived and organized its defences. In June 1920 General Wrangel led the Whites' last sally, into southern Russia from the Crimea, only to be beaten back. The evacuation of his followers by sea virtually ended the Civil War in November.

In the end it was their central position, their better generalship and their more positive-sounding political programme which brought victory to the Reds. When the frontiers were at last stabilized, Finland and the three Baltic countries had retained their independence of Russian rule. So too had Poland, after attacking Soviet territory in the spring of 1920 and then beating off Soviet counter-attacking armies which penetrated deep into Polish territory. Poland retained sizcable ethnically Belorussian or Ukrainian areas which had been part of the Polish-Lithuanian state in the eighteenth century. But the bulk of the Ukraine accrued to Moscow, as did the Caucasus and Transcaucasia, the incorporation of which was completed with the invasion of Menshevik-ruled Georgia by the Red Army in 1921. Not until 1922 did the Soviet government regain control over eastern Siberia.

Though the Civil War had been won by early 1921, Lenin's problems had only just begun, for the country lay in ruins, its industry, transport system and food-producing capacity shattered after six years of hostilities. An enormous task of reconstruction faced the government, and this at a time when the population was half-starved, half-frozen and more than half disillusioned with Soviet rule. A great peasant revolt broke out in the Tambov province south-east of Moscow. Worse still, ideologically, were strikes in Petrograd and a naval mutiny in the near-by island base of Kronstadt, events marking the disaffection of the very workers and sailors who had once formed the vanguard of Bolshevism.

V.I. Chapayev (right), Bolshevik Civil War hero, confers with a divisional commander at Nikolayevsk-Uralsky railway station.

'Beat the Whites with the Red Wedge'. A Bolshevik Civil War poster (1919–20) by El Lissitzky.

Lenin now turned against his former supporters the political skills and violence once used to eliminate Whites and rival socialists. The Kronstadt rebellion was put down by military force, as was the Tambov rising, and Communist Party dissidents were silenced. At the crucial Tenth Party Congress, which coincided with the Kronstadt rebellion in March 1921, Lenin officially banned opposition within the Party – but without sanctioning the arrest and execution of Party members, as later ordained by Stalin.

The Tenth Congress was not all rigour, for Lenin also introduced an important concession interpreted by some as a betrayal of communist principles: his New Economic Policy (NEP). This permitted a measure of private trade such as had been banned during the Civil War period. NEP was especially helpful to the peasants, permitting them to grow crops for the market instead of finding their produce confiscated at bayonet point by armed requisitioners – an all too common experience in the years 1918–20. But NEP represented only a tactical retreat during which the state retained its control over the commanding heights of heavy industry. The introduction of NEP was, moreover, closely followed by the great famine of 1921–22, which chiefly hit the peasantry, causing some five million deaths. This disaster was mitigated through foreign aid organized by the future President of the United States Herbert Hoover, and by the Norwegian Arctic explorer Fridtjof Nansen.

Progressively incapacitated from May 1922 onwards by a series of cerebral strokes, Lenin had at one time seemed most likely to be succeeded by Trotsky as leader or dictator. But it is not always an advantage to be quite so apparent an heir, as became clear shortly after Lenin's death on 21 January 1924. Far from falling to Trotsky, the mantle of leadership devolved on the diminutive, pock-marked Georgian Joseph Stalin, *né* Dzhugashvili. Though senior colleagues had tended to dismiss Stalin as a mediocrity, nonentity or 'grey blur', he in fact possessed vastly superior skill in the Soviet power game, of which he himself was inventing the rules as he went along. Stalin's rise to the status of unchal-lenged dictator coincided with the period of NEP (1921–28), and was the most important political development of that era.

Stalin's rise can only be understood in the arid context of the nascent Soviet Party/governmental structure: a system of interlocking committees so profuse as to bewilder even their most active members – excepting always Stalin him-self, the arch-bureaucrat.

The chief seat of power was the Politburo (Political Bureau) of the Com-munist Party Central Committee. This small body, only five strong during the Civil War and thereafter somewhat expanded, was nominally elected by the larger Party Central Committee, itself theoretically appointed by the periodical (at first roughly annual) Party Congresses, consisting of delegates themselves chosen – again in theory – by rank-and-file members. In practice this apparently democratic pyramid was turned on its head, for it was the top manipulators (notably Stalin himself) who chose the membership of the larger bodies, packing them with obedient supporters. Moreover, after 1921, any attempt by the rank and file to assert initiative fell foul of Lenin's ruling against dissension within the Party. Barely had communists high and low celebrated the destruc-tion of all other political parties before they were robbed in turn of freedom to manoeuvre. Within a few years they would also be robbed of their lives.

Alongside the Party hierarchy stood a similar three-tier governmental structure, wherein a small cabinet (the Soviet of People's Commissars) was – again theoretically – responsible to the larger Central Executive Committee, itself appointed by the still larger periodical All-Union Congresses of Soviets elected – partly indirectly – by the population at large. This governmental hierarchy was enshrined in two early constitutions, that of the RSFSR (1918) and that of the USSR (1923). But in neither of these was the Party, the true repository of power, even mentioned.

The relationship between Party and government was somewhat obscured by considerable overlapping between the two hierarchies at the very top. Lenin himself had combined chairmanship of the Soviet of People's Commissars (the top governmental post) with acknowledged leadership of the Party as key figure in the Politburo. All high officers of government were Party members, as also were most senior officers of the armed forces, diplomats, police officials and the like. Pre-eminent influence, however, tended to accrue to functionaries high in the Party 'apparatus': those whose principal office was within the Party organization itself, irrespective of any other post which they might also hold.

From the beginning of Soviet rule Stalin had been firmly ensconced in the top echelons of both Party and government. He had served on the Party Central Committee since 1912, and had been a member of the Politburo from its inception in October 1917. On the Bolshevik seizure of power he received the important governmental post of People's Commissar for Nationalities, which he held until the commissariat was wound up in early 1923. In 1920–22 Stalin also held a second commissariat: that of the Workers' and Peasants' Inspectorate, a body which was created to infuse efficiency into the state machine, and which gave him additional scope for extending his influence. Between 1923 and 1940 Stalin held no governmental posts, but concentrated on domi-nating the Party's central organs. Besides sitting on the Politburo he was a founder-member of the Organization Bureau, which helped to translate the Politburo's policies into action, while also being powerful on the Central Control Commission responsible for Party discipline. Finally, there was the supremely important post to which he was elected on 3 April 1922: that of General Secretary to the Party Central Committee. Stalin eventually built up his secretariat until it rivalled or eclipsed the very Politburo, though by then the relative weighting of the two bodies had become an academic problem – for one man wielded absolute power over both, besides also controlling a private secretariat of his own.

Stalin achieved his pre-eminence partly through patience in tackling dull chores scorned by the more 'brilliant' colleagues whom he later exterminated. Nor was his course all plain sailing. He passed through troubled waters in the winter of 1922–23, having risked defiance of the ailing Lenin by initiating independent policies. A serious quarrel developed over Stalin's high-handed treatment of the local Communist Party which came to power in his native Georgia after the overthrow by the invading Red Army of Georgian indepen-dence in February 1921. Stalin also quarrelled with Lenin's wife, Nadezhda

Moscow, 1920. A queue outside a food shop.

Krupsky. In December 1922–January 1923 Lenin marked his displeasure by dictating a political testament and codicil, in which he suggested that a way should be found to remove Stalin from the general secretaryship of the Party Central Committee, and to replace him with some other comrade more considerate. Lenin also wrote to Stalin threatening to sever personal relations owing to his rudeness to Nadezhda Krupsky. Such was Lenin's prestige that these statements would surely have involved Stalin's political extinction, had they ever been made officially public. But though the contents leaked abroad, Stalin's rivals and future victims Zinovyev and Trotsky collaborated in suppressing the matter at home when it came up for consideration in the Central Committee shortly after Lenin's death. Within a year or two Stalin's control of communications was such that he could suppress this damning material, which was eventually disclosed to the Twentieth Party Congress by Khrushchev in February 1956.

Though Stalin's main tactic was to pack committees with his own creatures, he also showed an aptitude for stratagems more overt. He promoted an extrava-gant cult of the deceased Lenin, investing that modest but verbose leader's voluminous *œuvre* (apart from such inconvenient material as the testament)

Lenin's funeral, 27 January 1924. Kamenev (left) and the Cheka chief Dzerzhinsky (on Kamenev's left) act as bearers.

with the authority of Holy Writ. On the eve of Lenin's funeral Stalin pronounced a bizarre oath of devotion to his defunct leader, intoned in a guttural Georgian accent and couched in the idiom of Orthodox liturgy familiar to the aspiring dictator from his student years at the Tiflis Theological Seminary. Lenin's embalmed corpse was deposited in a mausoleum in Moscow's Red Square as if he were a defunct Pharaoh rather than an apostle of materialism and scientific socialism. As a further tribute, the Soviet Union's second city was rechristened Leningrad.

Himself no impassioned ideologist, Stalin had the useful knack of inducing more ideologically inclined competitors to quarrel with each other. After Lenin's death he first allied himself in a ruling triumvirate with Zinovyev and Kamenev, whom he encouraged to abuse Trotsky – now pushed into the background. Trotsky's decline was partly due to so effortless a consciousness of his own superiority that he saw no need to fight back until it was too late. In 1925, by which time Trotsky had been virtually disarmed, Stalin was able to form a new alliance – directed against Zinovyev and Kamenev. This temporary quadrumvirate – with Bukharin, Rykov and Tomsky – represented right-wing policies: concessions to the peasantry and a comparatively slow evolution towards a socialist society along the lines of NEP. In keeping with this attitude,

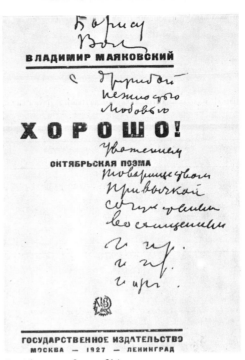

ВЛАДИМИР МАЯКОВСКИЙ

ХОРОШО!

ОКТЯБРЬСКАЯ ПОЭМА

ГОСУДАРСТВЕННОЕ ИЗДАТЕЛЬСТВО
МОСКВА — 1927 — ЛЕНИНГРАД

The poet Vladimir Mayakovsky (1894–1930) and (*right*) the title page of one of his poems, bearing an inscription to the writer Boris Pasternak.

Stalin enunciated his own policy as that of Socialism in One Country, thus staking his faith in the ability of the Soviet Union to 'go it alone', without waiting for world revolution. By now the prospects for world revolution seemed distant indeed – after unsuccessful attempts to foment it in Germany, China and elsewhere – so that Stalin's espousal of economic self-sufficiency was well timed to appeal to younger, more realistic, less ideologically-minded Party members and managers.

Stalin's rivals were outmanœuvred, each being pushed into ever less powerful positions within the Party, from which they were eventually expelled entirely. Among the landmarks in Zinovyev's fall were his replacement as Leningrad Party secretary by Stalin's protégé Kirov, and his removal from the chairmanship of the Comintern – the Soviet-dominated international communist organization founded in 1919. Trotsky had lost the post of Commissar for War as early as January 1925. By early 1928 he had been expelled from the Party altogether and exiled to Alma Ata in Central Asia – a prelude to banishment from the confines of the USSR. There followed a period of international wanderings during which Trotsky fulminated against Stalinism from alien hideouts until his skull was split open by the (presumably) Stalinist agent Ramon Mercader in a villa near Mexico City on 20 August 1940.

A train fitted out as a mobile school to tour remote districts of the Soviet Union. A photograph taken in the early 1920s.

COLLECTIVIZATION AND THE FIRST FIVE YEAR PLAN

Though Stalin had made himself *de facto* dictator by 1928, he was still operating through majority support within a Politburo which now contained nine members, his power being as yet far from absolute. Harshly as the USSR was administered, and hard as life was for the average citizen, conditions still remained pre-totalitarian. Police repression under the OGPU (the new title of the political security machine from 1923 onwards) was certainly severe, continuing to fall on non-communist socialists, religious practitioners and members of the pre-revolutionary privileged classes, while concentration camps engulfed many thousands of the régime's opponents. And yet, by comparison with the Cheka-operated terror of the Civil War, not to mention even worse ordeals which lay ahead, the incidence of state oppression was mild indeed. For instance, writers still enjoyed freedom to satirize Soviet society – as the works of Zoshchenko, and those of Ilf and Petrov, richly illustrate. Moreover, though direct attacks on the new governmental system were already dangerous, it was not yet obligatory to make positive affirmations of faith in Marx, Lenin, Stalin or any of their various doctrines. Between 1925 and 1927 the general standard of living had risen, and it seemed reasonable to face the future with optimism.

It was on such a comparatively placid community that Stalin, in 1928, launched a new revolution, imposed from above and fraught with changes yet more fundamental than those which had taken place in the first Soviet decade. The method was a crash programme of industrialization and regimentation replacing NEP and compelling the peasantry (numbering some twenty-five million individual homesteads) to amalgamate in collective and state farms.

The programme had urgent economic motives, since the Soviet Union seemed menaced by hostile capitalist states, while remaining a vulnerable, and still predominantly rural, community. During the first decade of Soviet rule life had changed surprisingly little in the Russian countryside. Inefficient small-scale farming still occupied a majority of the labour force, and some means must clearly be found of growing food more economically and of turning a proportion of the peasants into town-based factory workers. Yet, important as economic and military considerations were, Stalin's overriding motive was certainly political: the creation, at no matter what cost in human life and suffering, of a regimented society wholly dependent on himself.

Thus began the first phase of militant Stalinism, its main victims being the masses of the peasantry. Attached to individual farming as a way of life, and reinforced by centuries of traditional dumb resistance to authority, the peasants had no wish to become rural proletarians conscripted into village communities of about seventy-five households and termed collective or state farms. To break their resistance Stalin employed guile and force on an impressive scale. Cunning use was made of the opprobrious term 'kulak', traditionally applied to rustic usurers, but now officially defined to cover the minority of comparatively prosperous peasants – its use in practice being conveniently blurred to embrace any peasant opposed to collectivization. Decreeing the liquidation of the kulaks as a class, Stalin encouraged non-kulaks to loot their more prosperous or unpopular neighbours' property, and to expel them and their families from their homes. The process was calculated to split each village community, especially as there was no sure way of determining who was a kulak and who was not, though bluster, cunning and intrigue were helpful weapons in escaping persecution and diverting it to one's neighbours. By no means all peasants were prepared to tear each other apart, however, and collectivization was therefore further enforced by worker-activists drafted into the villages, as also by armed OGPU detachments and by units of the Red Army – including its air force – which machine-gunned, shelled or bombed the reluctant villagers. Collectivization was thus an undeclared war between the peasantry and Stalin, who was

171

later (in a much-quoted conversation with Winston Churchill) to calculate the number of his rustic victims at ten million. More recent scholarship has confirmed his very rough figure, adding that about a third of the peasants concerned were executed or perished from other causes, while a third were consigned to concentration camps and a further third were exiled without imprisonment. As part of the dual process of regimentation and industrialization the state established Machine Tractor Stations in the countryside. Besides mechanical aids, these also furnished a nucleus of Party and police officials who sought to carry Stalinist controls into every farmyard.

Tough and resourceful though they were, the peasants could not effectively resist so ruthless an onslaught. They retaliated by murdering officials and by burning their crops, as also by slaughtering their cattle and horses – on such a scale that agricultural livestock was reduced by about a half between 1928 and 1933. Yet some sixty per cent of peasant homesteads had been collectivized by 1932, when the First Five Year Plan was declared completed before time. The same year also saw the outbreak of the second great Soviet famine, in the Ukraine

A cartoon poster of 1929 depicting enemies of the First Five Year Plan, with some lines by the propagandist versifier Demyan Bedny.

Peasants are enrolled in collective farms: a scene from the early 1930s.

and along the Volga. It claimed some five million further peasant victims – deliberately sacrificed by Stalin, who continued to dump Soviet grain on world markets while those who had grown it were starving *en masse*. The new dictator was very largely successful in concealing this disaster from world opinion.

Harsh measures were simultaneously adopted in the industrial field. But industrialization was not enforced with a severity comparable to that inflicted on the terrorized countryside, and considerable enthusiasm was enlisted in the drive to turn the Soviet Union into a formidable industrial complex supposedly destined to overtake the capitalist West. But industrialization, like collectivization, was chiefly important to Stalin as an instrument with which to achieve increased totalitarian control. Labour discipline was tightened, the trade unions being converted into a major enforcement agency, while instant dismissal became the penalty for a single day's absence from work. The martial

173

cries of official cheer-leaders rang out over the industrial 'front', and an internal passport system was introduced – obliging all citizens to carry an identity card, as had been the case in Imperial times.

By 1930 Stalin's OGPU was swiftly overtaking the Leninist Cheka as an instrument of mass oppression. The concentration camp system was expanded to admit hordes of 'dekulakized' peasants, often transported in sealed, unheated freight wagons in the heart of winter, so that many were unloaded dead on arrival. A sufficient quantity survived, however, to compel the camps to cater for millions, whereas they had previously housed mere tens of thousands. Prisoners were drafted in bulk to Five Year Plan projects, such as the White Sea Canal on which some 300,000 worked under appalling conditions. Police operations of this kind were publicly misrepresented by gullible or mischievous notabilities, both native and foreign, as now a Bernard Shaw, now a Maxim Gorky volunteered praise for Stalin such as had become a constant accompaniment to his rule of terror. Though modest in dress, and often unassumingly jovial in manner, Stalin had (unlike Lenin) permitted a major city to be re-named after him in his own lifetime, when Tsaritsyn became Stalingrad in

A general view of the Dnieper dam, completed in 1932 as part of the first large Soviet hydro-electric station.

The building of the 'Turksib' (the Turkestan–Siberian railway), which connects the Trans-Siberian with the Tashkent–Orenburg line; it was completed in 1930.

1925. By his fiftieth birthday, on 21 December 1929, the dictator had become the object of a nation-wide cult. On walls, in houses and in offices, graven images and icons of the mustachioed leader were prominently displayed, while grossly fulsome articles in the press lauded his qualifications as a universal genius – and as one distinguished by his humane concern for the very subjects whom his minions were so busily starving, shooting and freezing all around him.

Among the police measures now practised was the use of torture to extract gold and jewellery hoarded by private citizens at a time when the Soviet Union sorely needed foreign exchange with which to buy machinery. The period also saw the first Stalinist show trials, for which the period of Lenin's rule had furnished a model in the trial, almost a political lynching, of certain Socialist Revolutionaries in 1922. As an apprentice trial-rigger on his own account, Stalin had managers and engineers indicted for sabotaging the Soviet industrial revolution. He thus created scapegoats on whom the innumerable deficiencies of the economy could be blamed, as first happened at the Shakhty trial in 1928, when over fifty engineers and technicians from the Donbass were accused of sabotage in the mines. Other trials followed, including that of the Metro-Vickers engineers at which British citizens were prominent among the alleged

wreckers. There was also a political trial of former Mensheviks. It is retrospec-
tively obvious that Stalin was now preparing for the judicial murder of leading
communists by first obtaining their consent to the framing of non-communists.
Already many features of the later Moscow trials (1936–38) were evident:
sedulously fostered hysteria, courts packed with pliant claques, processions of
screaming 'workers' on the streets, the rigging of evidence, the forced confessions and the participation of the sinister and ingenious Vyshinsky as judge or
prosecutor. These early experiments were to show their value to the full when
Stalin, flushed with his victory over the Russian peasant, set himself to destroy
the very political colleagues who had helped first Lenin and then himself to
power.

THE GREAT TERROR

In the years 1933–34 the Soviet Union at last seemed to be weathering the storm
of Stalinism. The Second Five Year Plan of 1933–37 appeared to promise a less
hectic life, the civil war against the peasants had been called off, and the great
famine of 1932–33 had been succeeded by comparative plenty. Though a
disastrous failure in its agricultural aspects, the First Five Year Plan had achieved
many of its industrial objectives. There had been a great increase in iron and
coal production, together with an expansion of the overloaded transport
system, now equipped with new canals, roads and railway lines. Other developments had included the building of a huge hydro-electric station on the River
Dnieper in the Ukraine. As for Stalin's main unavowed aim – the imposition
of totalitarian control – here the norm had indeed been over-fulfilled, to use a
phrase of the period. In keeping with these triumphs the Seventeenth Party
Congress of January–February 1934 was called the Congress of Victors. A
benign Stalin made sweeping claims for the success of his policies, maintaining
that there was 'nothing to prove and no one left to beat'. As a pledge of further
relaxation, the OGPU was wound up in July 1934, when political security
was placed under the milder-sounding People's Commissariat for the Interior
(NKVD).

That these initials would become synonymous with atrocities far more
widespread than those associated with Cheka and OGPU combined, no one
could yet suspect – for who could guess that the seemingly all-powerful Stalin
secretly found his thirst for power still unslaked? Meanwhile some of his senior
protégés were murmuring criticism of his policies, and pamphlets calling for his
removal were cautiously circulated. The anti-Stalin manifesto (1932) of one

Sergey Kirov. A photograph taken in 1934, the year of his assassination.

Ryutin especially alarmed the dictator, who characteristically bided his time while unobtrusively preparing to assault a new category of victims: members of the Communist Party which had been his own ladder to power. These had hitherto been subject to purges only in the physically painless sense of expulsion from their party, remaining relatively immune from arrest and imprisonment amidst all the horrors which they had eagerly sanctioned or administered. From execution they were still entirely safe. Stalin must break this last crucial taboo – must equip himself to order any execution at will – before he could become absolute master of the whole Soviet community.

Stalin's Great Terror may be traced back to 1 December 1934, the date on which an assassin fatally shot Sergey Kirov in the corridor of his Leningrad headquarters. Kirov had become a rising star of the Party. A member of the Politburo and the First Party Secretary (in effect Governor) of Leningrad Province, he had long been a protégé of Stalin's, but had recently developed certain inconvenient qualities. He was popular, being considered a potential successor to Stalin, and he was an advocate of comparative relaxation. His death at the hands of a disgruntled nonentity remains one of the many unsolved murder mysteries of Russian history. The assumption, mooted by Khrushchev in 1956, that Stalin ordered the killing through various intermediaries (among them the secret police chief Yagoda) has been widely accepted as plausible in view of the dictator's impressive criminal record. Kirov's death was certainly useful to Stalin, removing a leading rival, and providing the excuse for an orgy of reprisals which eventually included the execution or arrest (followed by exile) of thousands in Leningrad, a rival power-centre to Moscow. Guilt for Kirov's murder was also foisted on Zinovyev and Kamenev, who were now tried *in camera* and sentenced to terms of imprisonment.

Though this was all that Stalin could achieve in early 1935, he had by no means finished with Zinovyev and Kamenev, for it was his intention utterly to destroy these and other potent figures from the great Bolshevik past. He plotted to plunge them into total ignominy, and to parade them before the world crawling degradedly as they mouthed grovelling recantations at specially rigged show trials. They would then be shot, whereby a precedent would be set for the execution of Party members – even those with the most august credentials – and the dictator's powers would consequently know no bounds.

The three great Moscow show trials of 1936–38 became the main symbol and overt instrument of Stalin's drive for yet greater power. For these puzzling affairs judicial history provides few parallels apart from the Soviet pilot trials of 1928–33 mentioned above. The world was astonished that Bolsheviks of such stature as Zinovyev and Kamenev – and later Bukharin and Rykov – should behave so abjectly in the dock. Accusations levelled at the three trials, against a mixed bag of fifty-four defendants in all, included the assassination of Kirov, as also conspiracy to assassinate Stalin and other leaders. Among other charges were numbered wholesale sabotage of the Soviet economy, espionage for Germany, Britain and Japan, and plotting to restore capitalism in the USSR, of which large areas were allegedly to be ceded to Germany and Japan. The last of the three great show trials, that of Bukharin and twenty others in March 1938, presented especially grotesque details, though there was nothing *prima facie* implausible in the charge that the former OGPU and NKVD boss Yagoda had murdered his predecessor Menzhinsky and plotted the murder of his successor Yezhov. Except for some minor respects in which certain of the accused fell short of total co-operation with the prosecution, they all eagerly acknowledged their guilt, having been processed by threats and promises affecting their families, by physical ill-treatment, by pleas to make a final sacrifice for the sake of the Party and so on. These methods were applied by NKVD officials who were faced with similar treatment themselves (Yagoda and Yezhov actually received it) if the chief actors should forget or garble their lines in court.

Once Zinovyev and Kamenev had been shot, on 25 August 1936, Stalin was free to execute whomever he wished, having acquired an extended licence

The first five officers to be promoted to the newly created rank of Marshal of the Soviet Union in November 1935. Top: Budyonny, Blyukher. Below: Tukhachevsky, Voroshilov, Yegorov. Of these, Blyukher, Tukhachevsky and Yegorov were executed on Stalin's orders between 1937 and 1939.

to kill which he exploited to the full. The over-all number of those slaughtered in 1937–38 did not necessarily exceed the multi-million total of collectivization's victims in 1929–30. These new targets for liquidation were, however, drawn substantially from the educated and managerial section of the community. No longer was the unlettered muzhik the typical victim, for now many an indignant freighter of kulaks was hoist with his own petard – not undeservedly, it may be felt. The victims included industrial managers, civil servants, examining magistrates, legal officers and the very police tycoons who had been most active in inflicting similar persecution on others – in short, they included all who had helped to make Stalinism work. Nor could foreign communists, Comintern officials or senior officers of the Komsomol (Young Communist League) complain of unfair discrimination, since the executioner's bullet or the concentration camp claimed an equitable share within these categories too.

A savage campaign of terror also struck the armed forces, beginning with the announcement, on 11–12 July 1937, that Marshal Tukhachevsky and seven other high-ranking army officers had been sentenced for treason at a secret trial and executed. The ensuing attack on the army and navy removed tens of thousands of officers, including the majority of those who held the rank of colonel and above. Thus the Soviet Union's capacity to resist aggression was grievously impaired just when she was menaced by the growing power of Hitlerite Germany.

Stalin.

Since all senior persons, military or civilian, tended to belong to the Party, the new terror inevitably took an enormous toll among members of that organization. But it fell with particular severity on the Apparatus of full-time Party officials: provincial secretaries and the like. The following statistics well illustrate the catastrophic impact on leading communists: 1,108 of the 1,966 delegates to the Seventeenth Party Congress 'of Victors' (1934) were arrested and charged with counter-revolutionary crimes, while 98 of the 139 members of the Central Committee elected by that same Congress were shot, mainly in 1937–38. The danger did not prove quite so acute within the Politburo as within the ranks immediately below, for by 1939 six of the ten members of the 1934 Politburo were still at liberty. Three had died mysteriously, possibly murdered on Stalin's orders (Kirov, Kuybyshev and Ordzhonikidze), while only one – Kosior – had been avowedly executed.

Though the liquidation of card-holding communists gave the Great Terror of 1937–38 its special character, it would be misleading to suggest that they constituted the majority of its victims, or that the general public remained exempt. Far from it, for the onslaught fell on virtually all sections of the community: religious believers and atheists, Slavs and non-Slavs, illiterates and university professors, Stalin-lovers and Stalin-haters. It struck Moscow, Leningrad, the RSFSR as a whole, the Ukraine and Belorussia, as well as Caucasia and Central Asia, ranging from Minsk to Vladivostok, from the Arctic to the deserts. The very concentration camp commandants were kidnapped by Stalin's execution squads. No one could feel safe, though women, dotards and infants felt the brunt less than men in the prime of life, and rustics less than town-dwellers.

Another feature of the terror was the skilful use made of one power structure to attack another. Though security policemen were used in large numbers to arrest members of the Party Apparatus, the Party Apparatus was also used against the police – indeed, Nicholas Yezhov (head of the NKVD at the height of the terror) was himself a Party *apparatchik* by career. Yezhov too perished, as had the former NKVD chief Yagoda before him. As police chief Yezhov was succeeded by the more durable Georgian Lavrenty Beria, who held office from 1938 to 1953.

By the end of 1938 the main horrors were over, having claimed untold millions of victims, but the purpose of the operation defies explanation to this day. Was the terror an irrational game played by a mad and evil genius? Or a technique of making Russia safe for Stalin personally by creating universal fear? Breaking down trust between colleagues, relatives and friends, between husband and wife, between parents and children (since all were liable to denounce each other in this atmosphere of witch-hunt run riot), the terror made the entire population dependent on the supreme ruler. Another achievement was the extermination of virtually all those Old Bolsheviks who had once smiled at the dim Georgian bureaucrat's plodding ways, lack of ideological *élan* and fitness only for the mundane chores of office. Only in the late 1930s did the full complexity of Stalin's character emerge – when it was noted that the latest massacres had been ushered in by a new Constitution promulgated in December 1936. Thus, even as it was corralled for butchery, the quaking citizenry found itself guaranteed widespread civil rights such as freedom of speech, assembly and the press, besides which constituent republics of the Union retained their nominal entitlement to secede, while the very drafting of this spurious and cynical document was entrusted to Bukharin and Radek – each already an earmarked show-trial victim.

In the late 1930s Soviet foreign policy becomes a more prominent factor than hitherto. Not that the USSR had been inactive in foreign affairs even during the preceding period, for she had long been pursuing the dual task of subverting foreign governments through Kremlin-instructed local Communist Parties, and of seeking short-term advantages (including loans and trade agreements) from these same victims-designate. Whether motivated by capitalist greed – in conformity with Moscow's calculations – or not, foreign governments co-operated guardedly, according diplomatic recognition to their self-proclaimed destroyer. This process culminated in the recognition of the Soviet government by the USA under President Roosevelt in 1933.

One abiding feature of Soviet foreign policy has been the special hostility reserved for those foreigners who might be thought communism's natural allies within the 'bourgeois' states: members of other left-wing parties. Soviet representatives have, accordingly, often seemed happier sharing caviare with foreign millionaire-businessmen, who at least fit into Marxist demonology, than hob-nobbing with foreign socialist politicians, who do not – and whose hands may be embarrassingly calloused through physical toil, as unavowedly disdained by many a leader of the Soviet proletariat from Stalin and Molotov downwards. This posture was, however, temporarily abandoned from 1934 onwards, as Stalin embraced the tactics of the Popular Front. Impressed at last by the dangers of Hitlerism, after a period in which Moscow-instructed German communists had shown more hostility to other parties of the German left than to the Austrian demagogue, the USSR now joined the League of Nations, and began to push the various foreign communist parties into alliances with left-wing groups such as led, for example, to the Blum government of 1936–37 in France.

The Spanish Civil War of 1936–39 increased the Soviet Union's foreign involvements. But though she aided the Republicans in their struggle against General Franco, her intervention remained half-hearted, and was more than matched by Hitlerite and Italian aid to the other side. Instructing his exported generals to keep out of the firing line in Spain, Stalin also saddled that strife-worn country with agents of the Soviet NKVD. These liquidated non-communist left-wing organizations within the Republican ranks, especially in Catalonia, before they were recalled to Moscow and themselves liquidated.

Alarmed less by Franco's victory in Spain than by Hitler's annexation of Austria and Czechoslovakia, and by the German threat to Poland which

Vyacheslav Molotov, Stalin's principal aide, signs the Soviet-Nazi non-aggression pact in Moscow on 23 August 1939. Standing: Joachim von Ribbentrop, Hitler's foreign secretary (left, centre), and Stalin (right centre).

developed in 1939, the Soviet government agreed to consider an anti-Hitlerite alliance with Britain and France. But while pursuing open negotiations with London and Paris, the USSR was also conducting secret discussions with Berlin. The result was the Soviet-German Pact of 23 August 1939. It cleared the way for Hitler to invade Poland on 1 September, and made the Second World War inevitable.

After German armies had effectively smashed Polish resistance in the first fortnight of September 1939, Stalin ordered his forces to occupy eastern Poland. They thus seized an area already pre-empted by the USSR in a secret codicil to the Soviet-German Pact, whereby territory lying between the two would-be world-conquering colossi had been partitioned in advance of hostilities. In accordance with these clauses and later amendments to them, the Soviet Union proceeded to dominate Estonia, Latvia and Lithuania, extorting military bases and imposing assistance treaties. Attempts to intimidate the Finns were less successful, and the Soviet Union accordingly invaded Finland in November 1939, thus beginning the Soviet-Finnish Winter War. Gigantic Soviet armies

Finnish troops in action during the Soviet-Finnish Winter War of 1939-40.

eventually smashed the Mannerheim Line, but though they had prevailed against their tiny neighbour by February 1940, the operation dealt a severe blow to Soviet prestige owing to prolonged Finnish resistance against overwhelming odds. World opinion took note, assessing Soviet military potential as contemptible: a calculation later revealed to be erroneous. The immediate result of the Finnish defeat was the annexation by the USSR of certain strategic areas, while Finland as a whole retained her sovereignty. Later in the year the USSR annexed the three Baltic countries, also compelling Rumania to cede Bessarabia and northern Bukovina.

The Hitler-Stalin pact involved extensive economic and military co-operation. Stalin punctiliously supplied Germany with raw materials, thus helping her to evade the British blockade, while Germany's fulfilment of her undertakings to Russia was less conscientious. Yet, despite considerable running friction between Moscow and Berlin, Stalin may have believed that he had successfully staved off an attack on the Soviet Union such as had been foreshadowed in those pages of Hitler's *Mein Kampf* which proclaim the need for German expansion in the east. Stalin would not heed repeated warnings of the impending German onslaught furnished by Soviet and British intelligence sources, and appears to have ignored the enormous German military build-up on his western borders in spring 1941.

At 4 a.m. on 22 June 1941 Hitler's forces struck simultaneously along the Soviet frontier running between the Baltic and the Black Seas. Even by the standards of the *Wehrmacht* which had so swiftly smashed French military power twelve months previously, initial German successes against Russia were spectacular. Within a few days much of the Soviet air force had been destroyed on the ground, while Nazi tanks ploughed deep into Soviet territory, making great encircling movements which led to the capture of Red Army prisoners by their hundred thousand. In many areas the advancing Germans were greeted as liberators, for it was expected that they would permit the conquered Soviet peoples, especially the Belorussians and Ukrainians in the first instance, to escape serfdom on collective farms and to practise their ancestral religion freely.

Within a few weeks the outcome of this super-*Blitzkrieg* might well have been settled in Hitler's favour, had it not been for the breakdown of the political and military 'genius' to which he apparently owed his earlier triumphs. Hitler's

Moscow, November 1941. Muscovites prepare anti-tank obstacles as German forces threaten the city's approaches.

Soviet partisans awaiting execution by the German occupying forces.

major strategic error was a failure to perceive the overriding importance of Moscow as a prime target, and a tendency to dissipate his efforts against other goals which included Leningrad, Stalingrad and Caucasian oil. He also tended (as did Stalin too) to insist on his troops clinging to conquered territory at all costs, even when tactical considerations made local retreat seem imperative to generals on the spot. Such mistakes helped to render superior German generalship ultimately ineffective.

Hitler committed a further blunder by treating the Soviet peoples, both Slav and non-Slav, as lesser breeds without the law, deliberately starving prisoners-of-war by the million, conscripting captured *Untermenschen* into labour gangs, shooting hostages and exterminating Jews. That Hitler outdid even Stalin in atrocities committed in occupied Soviet territory – especially by the SS and Gestapo – is an eloquent illustration of the carpet-biting Austrian's talent for inspiring cruelty. The natural effect was to rally the Soviet peoples around even a Stalin. If, as has been said, Hitler was the only person whom Stalin ever trusted, that trust did eventually pay off in an unexpected way: in the end Hitler's attack left the Soviet Union and its leader far stronger than before.

Though Soviet troops surrendered to the Germans *en masse* in certain areas, others resisted heroically from the outset, their efforts being backed by a growing partisan movement in the German rear. In effect the war was possibly lost by

The bodies of Soviet villagers massacred by German occupying troops.

Left: Fighting in the rubble of Stalingrad, November 1942. *Right:* Villagers prepare food in the stove of a ruined house on the Soviet western front.

Hitler as early as December 1941, when he failed to take Moscow despite repeated attacks pressed on with great determination. Stalin ordered the evacuation of government departments and diplomatic missions to Kuybyshev in the east, himself remaining in the Kremlin all along as an emblem of defiance and earnest of future victory. After briefly penetrating Moscow's suburbs, the Germans reeled back under the blows of massive Soviet reserves unexpectedly committed in ferocious winter weather, for which Teutonic troops proved worse adapted and clothed than Siberian.

The Germans returned to the attack in 1942, advancing deep into the northern Caucasus, but their cutting edge was fatally blunted in the winter of that year through an insensate, strategically unjustified attempt, enforced by Hitler, to hold the rubble of shattered Stalingrad on the lower Volga. It was here that the Germans, routed and enveloped in vast numbers, sustained their first major defeat of

Soviet tanks attack in the Ukraine.

the war. From early 1943 onwards the tide began to turn against them in the world at large, as well as on Soviet territory.

Between October 1943 and November 1944 seven Soviet minority nationalities (some of which had been briefly overrun by the Germans) were deported *en masse* on Stalin's orders to remote regions of Asiatic Russia, collaboration or sympathy with the invader being presumably one of the motives which inspired these harsh measures. The peoples concerned were the Chechens, the Ingushes, the Karachays, the Balkars and the Meshketians (all denizens of the Caucasus), as also the Kalmyks and Crimean Tatars. The total number of individuals thus savagely uprooted, with great loss of life, was over a million.

Through her alliance with the USA and Britain, the USSR received enormous quantities of military equipment, but too little of what Stalin considered direct military assistance. From the outset he had called for the opening of a second front through an invasion of German-held France by his western allies. The delay by Britain and the USA in providing such support became a source of diplomatic friction. By the time of the Normandy landings in June 1944 the Red Army was already threatening to push the *Wehrmacht* back into German national territory. In May of the following year Soviet troops took Berlin, shortly after Hitler's suicide, and all Germany was occupied by the victorious Allies. On 8 August 1945, two days after the United States air force had dropped an atomic bomb on Hiroshima, the USSR declared war on Japan. The Japanese surrender followed on 2 September. With hard-won victory in the west and easily won success in the east, Stalin had now avenged the Russian defeat of 1904–05 as well as that of 1914–18.

Even before the outbreak of hostilities, Stalin had almost thrown away any chance of victory, for he had not only drastically weakened the Red Army through the purge of its officer corps in 1937–38, but had also failed to arm his country and to organize it adequately during the breathing space gained by the Soviet-German Pact of 1939. Yet he did possess one valuable asset which his Austrian opponent either lacked or had lost: an ability to learn from his own mistakes. Above all, Stalin acquired the art of effective delegation to such competent generals as George Zhukov, whose success as wartime army commander earned him widespread popularity in the Soviet Union – but also, typically, relegation to a minor regional command when hostilities were over.

During the war Stalin largely abandoned Marxist ideological appeals in order to foster Great Russian patriotic sentiment such as he had already been favouring in the 1930s. It was less the paladins of early Marxism than such ancient native heroes as Alexander Nevsky and Dmitry Donskoy – together with Minin and Pozharsky (ousters of Poles in the Time of Troubles) and the Imperial Russian generals Suvorov and Kutuzov – who now became the objects of official adulation. Persecution of the Orthodox Church was relaxed, its support being recruited for the Soviet war effort. Such postures may have been more than mere political expediency on Stalin's part, for by now this Georgian former student of theology had embraced Russian patriotism, and the traditional aims of Imperial Russian foreign policy, with a fervour worthy of any native Muscovite. The emphasis on Russian nationalism helped to persuade the other Allies that the USSR had abandoned the goal of world revolution, and was pursuing the less alarming policy of Russian self-interest instead. By dissolving the Comintern in 1943 (but without abandoning control of foreign Communist Parties), Stalin deliberately encouraged this impression.

The Red Flag is erected on the roof of the Reichstag in Berlin, 8 May 1945. ▶

The last phase of Stalinism (1945–53) much disappointed all who had hoped for continued co-operation between the Soviet Union and her wartime allies. Also disappointed was the Soviet population, which longed for relaxation even as Stalin resumed domestic repressions temporarily eased during hostilities. Moreover, the period witnessed the extension and consolidation of Muscovite sway over seven countries of eastern Europe – though one of these countries, Yugoslavia, escaped in 1948 – and over part of an eighth (eastern Germany). Two world camps, one headed by the USA and the other by the USSR, were separated by an Iron Curtain and became embroiled in a Cold War for which each side repeatedly blamed the other during the ensuing quarter of a century.

Four years of savage warfare, unparalleled in scale, had wrought fearful havoc on Soviet soil. Some twenty million or more citizens of the USSR may have perished, and as many had been rendered homeless. To repair the damage new Five Year Plans, the Fourth (1946–50) and Fifth (1951–55), were adopted when the system of quinquennial planning, suspended during the war, was revived. The post-war plans were successful in restoring heavy industry, of which the centre of gravity had now moved eastwards, but the severe shortage of consumer goods was only marginally relieved, while the housing situation too remained desperate. In keeping with the general rigours, discipline was re-asserted on the collective farm. During the war privately worked peasant plots had been illicitly expanded with tacit official consent, but were now cut down to size. There was also a considerable amalgamation of collective farms until the total number was reduced: from about a quarter of a million to less than a hundred thousand in 1952. The period also saw the end of the People's Commissariats, as first constituted in 1917. In 1946 they were renamed Ministries, the People's Commissars becoming Ministers. As part of this process the NKVD was automatically re-entitled the MVD.

German prisoners of war are paraded in the streets of Moscow.

Returning Red Army soldiers are welcomed in Moscow.

The last-mentioned change of name betokened no loosening of control. Even during hostilities internal repression had only been slightly relaxed, and the vast concentration-camp empire had played a major part in supporting the Soviet wartime economy. Meanwhile the fiction that no such camps existed was still officially maintained, though the number of inmates may well have exceeded a mean of ten million – a total constantly depleted owing to the high mortality rate, but constantly replenished by batches of newly freighted slave workers.

In 1945 the Red Army's victories in Europe had created a situation similar to that following Napoleon's defeat by Imperial Russia in 1812–14. On both occasions Russian troops felt that their sufferings and victories entitled them to a greater degree of freedom after their return home – aspirations which Stalin set himself to stamp out even more ruthlessly than had Alexander I. Extensive screening was applied to all who had been exposed to contagion from the polluting foreigner, whether of German, British, American or any other nationality, a high, though unknown, proportion of the screened being arrested and sent to camps. A soldier's capture by the Germans was equated with desertion, and among the minority of Soviet prisoners-of-war who survived many suffered transfer from Hitlerite to Stalinist slave camps. Similar treatment was inflicted on Soviet civilians who had been deported to the Reich as forced labourers and on partisans who had fought against the Germans. Other Soviet citizens (totalling scores of millions), who had somehow survived German occupation, were also subjected to investigation, and large numbers of them were arrested. All these

193

categories provided freshly enslaved recruits for Beria's concentration camps. Nor were the Soviet authorities content to have laid hands on the many millions recovered through the Red Army's advances. On the basis of the Yalta agreement of 1945 they compelled the USA, Britain, France and other countries forcibly to repatriate many of the Soviet citizens found within their jurisdiction. Though some were willing to return, many were not, suspecting what fate awaited them. Despite desperate unarmed resistance and numerous spectacular suicides, forcible repatriation continued until some two million had been sent back: a unique example of co-operation by democratic countries in the police measures of totalitarianism. About half a million Soviet citizens evaded repatriation and established themselves in non-communist countries.

Intensified police measures were accompanied by a harsh ideological campaign directed by Stalin's close associate Zhdanov, who opened fire in August 1946 with an attack on two well known writers, Zoshchenko and Anna Akhmatov, for displaying insufficient political militancy in their works. The drive for greater ideological rigour then broadened, embracing representatives of the entire Soviet intellectual spectrum from composers of music to geneticists. Strident assertion of Party dogma was combined with frenzied insistence on Great Russian racial supremacy purportedly incarnated in such feats as the invention of the steam engine and radio in advance of Watt and Marconi by Russians hitherto obscure. The campaign involved the denunciation of all who 'kow-towed to the West' – for instance, through lack of zeal in blackguarding the USA, now branded as Moscow's arch-enemy. After Zhdanov's death in 1948 the witch-hunt gathered force, acquiring an anti-Semitic note in the use of the derisive phrase 'rootless cosmopolitans' as a synonym for Jews. But despite many distasteful details the drive was less lethal than the Yezhov terror of 1937–38, being geared to recantations, not to slaughter.

The 1941–45 conflict extended the Soviet Union's western frontiers up to or beyond those of the Russian Empire as it had been in 1914, except that Finland retained her independence after making certain territorial concessions. Estonia, Latvia and Lithuania were reincorporated as constituent republics of the USSR. Territories which had been part of pre-war eastern Poland were annexed or re-annexed to the Belorussian or the Ukrainian Republic. Bukovina too went to the Ukraine, while Bessarabia went to form the Moldavian Republic. The Soviet Union also took Kaliningrad (formerly Königsberg) and part of what had been East Prussia, besides extracting certain concessions from the Japanese in the far east.

Left: The 'Big Three' (Churchill, Roosevelt and Stalin) at Yalta during their conference of February 1945. *Right:* Truman (centre), Stalin (second from left) and Churchill (right foreground) on 17 July 1945 during the conference at Potsdam.

Soviet control was also extended, well beyond the area once ruled by the Romanovs, to the seven countries of eastern Europe which – together with Soviet-occupied eastern Germany – became known as Soviet satellites. The process of foisting Muscovite domination on a hundred million people – Albanians, Bulgarians, Czechoslovaks, eastern Germans, Hungarians, Poles, Rumanians and Yugoslavs – was complicated, involving varied combinations of intimidation and guile. Poland caused the most difficulty, but also became the precedent which helped to topple the others. Yugoslavia had made her own revolution, unlike the others, while for a time Albania seemed more of a Yugoslav than a Soviet satellite. East Germany, the post-war Soviet zone of occupation, was converted into the German Democratic Republic in 1949. Though each satellite was a special case, the handling of these countries by Moscow presented many common features. Ruthless economic exploitation was combined with Soviet police controls applied through nominally independent local security forces and Communist Parties. Despite these measures the satellites all retained some degree of autonomy by comparison with the component republics of the USSR.

Of the potential dangers presented by even minimal autonomy Stalin received warning when Yugoslavia broke free from Moscow in 1948. This occurred shortly after the establishment of the Cominform – a successor to the Comintern, but containing nine Communist Parties only – to co-ordinate the satellite camp. The main cause of the Soviet-Yugoslav quarrel was Marshal Tito's refusal to accept the extreme colonial status imposed on Belgrade by

195

Moscow. Unable to destroy Tito by vituperation, yet unwilling to use force, Stalin had to tolerate this major defection and to see a leading satellite accept limited association with the West.

To ensure that Titoist contamination should not spread was now vitally important. Stalin accordingly proceeded to drill the other satellite governments and Communist Parties in the ritual of servility by forcing them to stage show trials such as had once brought Zinovyev and Bukharin to their doom at home. Leading satellite communists were accordingly arrested, processed, publicly displayed in grovelling postures and executed or imprisoned in Budapest, Sofia, Warsaw, Prague and Tirana. National deviationism – that is, resistance to Soviet control – was prominent among the charges, and the much publicized courtroom confessions intimidated the surviving leaders who had been compelled to stage these degrading pageants while themselves in peril of similar disgrace.

Thus Stalin contained satellite restiveness from 1948 onwards, himself restrained from further expansion by resistance to Soviet imperialism on the part of the western powers under United States leadership. Attempts to extend Soviet control to Greece, South Korea and to the Allied sectors of Berlin foundered on such varied but effective obstacles as the Truman Doctrine, United Nations military intervention and a massive air-lift. On the global stage these western defensive victories were dwarfed by the establishment of communist rule over China in 1949. Yet, dependent though she was on Russian aid at the outset, and great as was the acclaim belatedly accorded to her revolution by Moscow, People's China never seemed destined for true satellite status, if only because her population was more than double that of the USSR.

STALIN'S HEIRS

The Nineteenth Party Congress met in October 1952. It was the first such gathering since 1939, being ten years overdue: an indication of the extent to which Stalin had abandoned even the pretence of ruling through Party or governmental organs. The Nineteenth Congress was remarkable for the leading role assigned to George Malenkov, long a close associate of the ageing dictator and now paraded as heir apparent. Meanwhile the police chief Beria had seemingly been scheduled for liquidation in a new great terror. One sign of Stalin's intention to launch such a holocaust was the dissolution of the eleven-man Politburo and its replacement by a Presidium of twenty-five members. The original members of the Politburo stayed, but found themselves sitting alongside a majority of upstarts. That the dictator intended this arrangement as a

At the funeral of the Soviet leader Michael Kalinin in 1946. Left to right: Bulganin (with arm band), Mikoyan, Beria, Malenkov, Stalin, Molotov, Kaganovich, Zhdanov.

prelude to the liquidation of the older stratum – and, eventually, of the newer too – is generally agreed by students of his methods.

By another decision of the Nineteenth Congress the time-honoured word Bolshevik was dropped from the Party's official title, which was now altered to 'Communist Party of the Soviet Union'. The change set the seal on Stalin's virtual destruction of the men who had made the October Revolution of 1917.

That the paranoid leader indeed planned a new terror became more evident in January 1953, when it was announced that nine Kremlin doctors – between four and seven of them (according to varying reports) being Jewish – had been arrested for procuring the murder of high functionaries, including Zhdanov, by medical means. Accompanied by strident calls for greater vigilance – always a reliable storm signal – the 'investigation' of the Doctors' Plot (in fact a fabrication of Stalin's police) appeared to menace everyone in the dictator's entourage, and ultimately the country as a whole. Then the menace collapsed with the announcement, on 6 March 1953, that Stalin had died of a stroke on the previous evening. Whether murdered (as has been suspected) or not, the septua-genarian universal genius was embalmed and placed on show by Lenin's side in the Red Square mausoleum. His demise makes 1953 the most important single year in Soviet history. Owing to a notable reduction in state-imposed terror, which has nevertheless remained a powerful background factor, the dictator's death changed the general tone of Soviet life, replacing quivering fear with wary apprehension.

One immediate outcome of Stalin's death was a dynastic crisis which evokes memories of many similar *contretemps* in earlier Russian history. At first the succession seemed to be clearly settled in favour of Malenkov. On 7 March he assumed the two main offices held by Stalin during his last years: the leading secretaryship of the Party Central Committee and the prime ministership (that is, the chairmanship of the Soviet of Ministers). But one week later Malenkov relinquished his party secretaryship to Nikita Khrushchev. The front-runner was already flagging.

The next dynastic crisis occurred in June 1953 with the arrest of Beria, the second most powerful figure in the leadership after Malenkov. Beria's control of the security forces, including entire police armies, had made him especially dangerous to all his rivals, and in December of the same year it was announced that he had been secretly tried and executed, together with six other leading security tycoons of the Stalin era. As this episode illustrates, the powers of the security police were trimmed after Stalin's death, but though the organization was brought under closer control by the Party, it retained considerable powers under its new title of KGB (Committee of State Security) from 1954 onwards.

By late 1953 Khrushchev had notably strengthened his position, his title having been changed from that of 'Secretary' to that of 'First Secretary' of the Party Central Committee. The most mentally agile among various competing potentates, he managed to discredit Malenkov's policy of simultaneously seeking international relaxation and emphasizing the primacy of consumer goods at home. In February 1955 Malenkov, by now outmanœuvred, asked to be relieved of the prime ministership, the post going to Khrushchev's temporary ally Bulganin. But Malenkov still retained his membership of the Presidium.

Having dislodged Malenkov, Khrushchev revealed a Stalin-like flexibility by switching from a hard-line policy to the sponsorship of international and domestic relaxation such as had been associated with the ousted Prime Minister. Khrushchev visited Belgrade with Bulganin in 1955 in an endeavour to compose the long-standing quarrel with President Tito. Then, at the Twentieth Party Congress in February 1956, the First Secretary delivered a momentous speech: 'secret', but soon leaked abroad, and unprecedented in the outspokenness with which Stalin's record was attacked on a Soviet official occasion.

Though disclosing many new details, the Secret Speech contained no major revelations about Stalin's character. Its real interest lay in the fact that a Soviet leader had at last admitted, however privily, what was already common knowledge: that the deceased dictator had used torture and police terror against his political associates. Stalin was also blamed for inept wartime leadership and for the quarrel with Tito. Khrushchev was careful neither to besmirch Stalin's early (pre-1934) reputation nor to attack the collectivization of agriculture. Nor did the budding despot denounce Stalin's repression of so many million humble citizens who had never been members of his party.

To describe the many calamities of the Terror a soothing formula had been devised: 'phenomena associated with the cult of the personality of J. V. Stalin'. Among such phenomena the concentration-camp system was by no means dismantled after Stalin's death, but conditions were somewhat eased, a significant though unknown number of inmates being released. Certain carefully selected individuals, slain or proscribed by the Stalinist state, were officially 'rehabilitated'.

In a world ever eager to console itself by exaggerating the importance of Soviet thaw symptoms such developments combined with Khrushchev's carefully dosed abuse of Stalin to earn him an international reputation as a liberal-minded reformer. Yet even at the time a minority of observers could sense that this smiling, bouncing, clubbable little *faux bonhomme* was no champion of liberal values, but rather one who used liberal postures as a lever in the power struggle.

One by-product of Khrushchev's policies was unrest among the east European satellites in autumn 1956. In the wake of riots and popular pressure the Polish communist leader Gomulka (disgraced and imprisoned in Stalin's day for Titoist inclinations) was brought to power in Warsaw against Moscow's wishes, and despite a sudden pounce on the Polish capital made by Khrushchev in person as part of an attempt to reassert Soviet control. In Hungary a full-scale October Revolution broke out, leading to an attempt by a new Hungarian government to withdraw from the Warsaw Pact: the military agreement binding the USSR and her satellites which had been signed in the previous year. The Hungarian rebellion was suppressed by Soviet tanks, but the outbreak laid Khrushchev open to criticism by Party hard-liners. Meanwhile, in the Soviet Union itself, intellectual dissidence had become more vocal than at any time since the 1920s. The jocular First Secretary curbed such strivings too, but once again appeared responsible for having provoked them in the first place.

Khrushchev was especially vulnerable in June 1957, when he found himself in a minority on the Presidium, which had been reduced in membership immediately after Stalin's death. Outvoted by Stalinist hard-liners – including the trio Molotov, Kaganovich and Malenkov, who were now united against

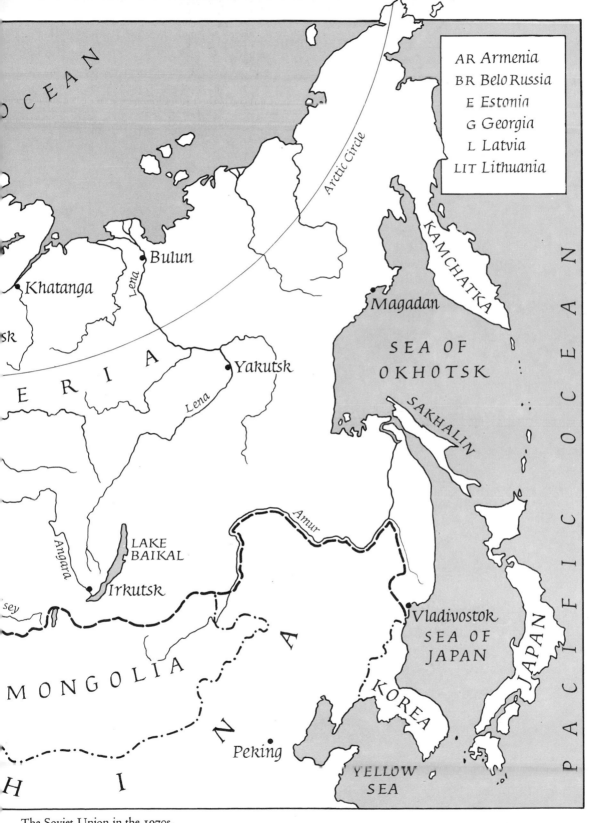

The Soviet Union in the 1970s.

Legend:
AR Armenia
BR Belo Russia
E Estonia
G Georgia
L Latvia
LIT Lithuania

him – the First Secretary yet turned potential disaster into triumph. He success-fully appealed over the heads of his fellow Presidium members to the Central Committee, which he had long been packing with his own nominees. The resulting *coup d'état* firmly established his pre-eminence, while compassing the political extinction of Malenkov, Molotov and Kaganovich, now pilloried as leaders of an Anti-Party Group. Other leading figures followed them into disgrace. Marshal Zhukov had come to Khrushchev's assistance in June 1957, but was himself dropped later in the same year, while Bulganin's down-fall followed in early 1958. When, in March of that year, Khrushchev assumed the prime ministership alongside his post of First Secretary, his ascendancy over all rivals had been assured. As was noted with relief both at home and abroad, the disgrace of Khrushchev's rivals did not lead to their physical elimination. They received minor appointments, even retaining their Party membership.

That Stalin was indeed dead such lenient treatment of fallen power-seekers did most eloquently emphasize. Nor did Khrushchev himself contrive to assume Stalinist powers during the remainder of a reign which lasted for another six and a half years, until October 1964. He was forced to maintain his supremacy by dominating a small ruling oligarchy (the Presidium) and its larger support-ing base (the Central Committee) while continuing to angle for greater power by simulating liberal postures. The Twenty-Second Party Congress of 1961 became the scene for renewed attacks on Stalin's memory, and provoked the summary removal of the embalmed despot from the Red Square mausoleum.

As that episode well illustrates, Khrushchev's style of leadership depended heavily on the public gesture. Flamboyant and publicity-minded, he offered a spectacular contrast to the taciturn Stalin – always a doer rather than a talker. Khrushchev also sponsored what became known, after his downfall, as 'hare-brained schemes', such as the project of ploughing up huge areas of virgin land in Kazakhstan and Siberia in order to solve the food problem. After initial successes this grandiose project turned sour owing to erosion and other factors. At one period in 1963 the Soviet Union was even reduced to importing grain in quantity: a disgrace indeed for a country which had been a leading grain-exporter in Imperial times. Khrushchev was continually tinkering with the structure of administration, now splitting the Party into agricultural and indus-trial segments, now sponsoring the decentralization of economic control. Each ushered in by raucous publicity fanfares, nostrum succeeded gimmick and panacea nostrum with bewildering rapidity. Among his uglier enact-ments was an extension of the death penalty to cover economic crimes, several

Nikita Khrushchev and Mrs Jacqueline
Kennedy, wife of the American
President, at a reception held in Vienna
to mark the Kennedy-Khrushchev
talks of summer 1961.

hundred persons (many with identifiably Jewish surnames) being shot for such offences as the embezzlement of state property. Mob law was encouraged by the mass enrolment of state-sponsored vigilantes to combat hooliganism, and also by the establishment of 'comrades' courts', whereby rigged assemblies of workers were empowered to inflict penalties on their fellows by acclamation. Meanwhile laws against social parasitism made it possible for vocal busybodies to victimize anyone who could be stigmatized as an idler. The persecution of religious practitioners was also intensified.

For good or ill Khrushchev created a new climate in foreign relations. He threw open the Soviet frontiers to foreign tourists, also sponsoring cultural exchange – again in contrast with the quarantine imposed by Stalin. Foreigners ignorant of the Russian language were now shepherded around museums, exhibitions and the ornate Moscow underground railway network by smiling Soviet plain-clothes police agents. Meanwhile Khrushchev was pursuing his diplomatic goals by conducting, in effect, a global whistle-stop tour which included countries as various as India, China, Britain, France, the USA, the Scandinavian nations and the various satellites. Much prized by journalists for his stock of salty peasant wisecracks, he visited the United Nations and staged a demonstration by banging his shoe on the table during an official session – thus incurring the feared charge of lack of culture at home, where he was far from popular. Summit talks with Presidents Eisenhower and Kennedy, and also with other western leaders, principally revolved around the post-war status of Germany, but led to few tangible results.

A poster showing the first Soviet manned earth satellite and the cosmonaut Yury Gagarin who, on 12 April 1961, became the first man to orbit the Earth.

The Khrushchev era was also remarkable for its technological triumphs. The first Soviet atomic bomb having been exploded back in 1949, the first Soviet hydrogen bomb followed in August 1953. In 1957 the first successful test of a Soviet intercontinental ballistic missile took place, and on 4 October of the same year the first earth satellite, the Sputnik, was launched by Soviet scientists. On 1 May 1960 the Soviet defence system achieved a different sort of triumph by bringing down an American U2 reconnaissance plane near Sverdlovsk in the Urals. Discrediting Khrushchev's policy of seeking a *détente* with President Eisenhower, this episode weakened the First Secretary's position at home. His status was further undermined when President Kennedy thwarted a Soviet attempt to establish missile bases on Cuba by outfacing Khrushchevite bluster in October 1962.

Though Soviet triumphs in space research had continued, the orbiting of the first manned space satellite in April 1961 being a spectacular landmark, other factors weakened Khrushchev's position. Prominent among them was a serious breach with Communist China, which came into the open in the early 1960s. When China openly defected from the Muscovite power system, taking the baby satellite Albania with her, it became even clearer that there was no longer one homogeneous Kremlin-dominated world communist movement, as in Stalin's day. The former monolith had given way to 'polycentrism', Moscow being now rivalled not only by Peking, but also by Belgrade, Bucharest or even Tirana – and potentially, indeed, by any communist leader outside the eastern bloc who might choose to take an independent line.

A statesman of great audacity, Khrushchev had managed the Soviet Union like some agile juggler who dazzles his audience by keeping a wide variety of flashing objects airborne. In the end his confidence exceeded his balance and the multi-coloured gew-gaws collapsed with him. His sudden deposition (by the no longer tame Presidium during his absence on holiday at Sochi on the Black Sea) took the world and himself by surprise in October 1964. He was succeeded in his two main positions by a less flamboyant duumvirate, Leonid Brezhnev assuming the office of First Secretary and Alexis Kosygin that of Prime Minister.

KHRUSHCHEV'S HEIRS

Contrary to the predictions of those who expected a single autocrat to emerge, as after Lenin's death and then Stalin's, the Brezhnev-Kosygin team presided over the ruling oligarchy from October 1964 into the 1970s. Of the duumvirs Brezhnev was in effect the senior, being Party leader. At the Twenty-Third Party Congress of March 1966 he consolidated his personal position when he was elected General Secretary to the Party Central Committee – the title previously held by Stalin alone. At the same time the Presidium reverted to the older name Politburo, another Stalinist tradition being deliberately revived.

As these changes indicate, Brezhnev and Kosygin were pursuing a policy of cautious restalinization. A feature of their rule, comparatively welcome to all except foreign journalists, was its less rumbustious tone. This change was a tacit criticism of government by tantrum, as practised by Khrushchev – who was permitted to live peaceably in retirement. Many of Khrushchev's experiments

The conclusion of the twenty-fourth Soviet Communist Party Congress in April 1971. From left to right: Leonid Brezhnev, General Secretary of the Soviet Communist Party; Nicholas Podgorny, Chairman of the Presidium of the Supreme Soviet; Alexis Kosygin, Prime Minister; Michael Suslov, Secretary of the Central Committee.

were quietly dropped and a more stable life began. Yet neither in agriculture nor in industry did the abandonment of political juggling inspire the required tempos, for though Soviet economic growth was maintained, it came to lag behind that of such capitalist pace-setters as Japan and West Germany.

Intensified persecution of intellectual dissidents was a marked feature of domestic policy. The trial of the writers Sinyavsky and Daniel in February 1966, based on alleged anti-Soviet material contained in works published abroad, was only one act of persecution among many affecting intellectuals. Widespread repression was also directed against religious practitioners, and against representatives of minority nationalities – especially Ukrainians, but also Crimean Tatars and many others – who sought to reduce the impact of Great Russian overlordship. Successive acts of oppression provoked protests, the protesters themselves then becoming the martyrs commemorated in the next protest wave. Much of the protest material filtered abroad, publicizing such atrocious practices as that of confining political dissidents in mental wards supervised by doctors under police orders. Numerous illicit typescripts were privily circulated in the Soviet Union and smuggled abroad. Beside publicistic material, they also included *belles lettres*, Alexander Solzhenitsyn's long novels *Cancer Ward* and *The First Circle* being outstanding.

The Brezhnev-Kosygin period saw an attempt by the Czechoslovak government and Party under Alexander Dubček to throw off colonial status. After long delays the Soviet army and other Warsaw Pact forces invaded defiant Czechoslovakia on 20–21 August 1968, this being the first of a series of measures which eventually resulted in the reimposition of an administration subservient to the Kremlin.

In the world at large the greatest extension of Soviet power occurred in the Middle East, where Moscow consolidated a stranglehold on Egypt and other Arab states by supplying them with arms for use against Israel – a policy which goes back to the Suez crisis of 1956 and before. By maintaining naval units in the Mediterranean, as well as in the Indian Ocean and on the world's seaways at large, Moscow asserted its power beyond the bounds set in the Khrushchev and Stalin eras. The Soviet space programme continued – outshone by manned American landings on the moon in 1969 – as also did the armaments drive, with much emphasis on protection against ballistic missiles.

Reviewing Soviet achievements in the early 1970s, one must salute the success with which both armaments and heavy industry have been built up over the years, and also the political skill with which the population has been

The guns of Soviet tanks temporarily halted on the streets of Prague during the Soviet invasion of Czechoslovakia in the summer of 1968.

induced to strengthen the state by forgoing standards of individual prosperity and civil liberty such as are widely taken for granted in the western world. The Soviet government is also to be admired for its skill in developing new techniques of colonial rule appropriate to an age in which traditional methods have proved wanting. By these procedures – which include the skilled use of ideology and propaganda, as well as of subservient, gullible and career-minded natives – the constituent republics of the USSR and the satellites have been kept under firm Russian control. Meanwhile, in other quarters of the globe, colonial peoples separated from their mother countries by salt water, and denied the cohesion imparted by an officially imposed mythology, have largely lapsed into independence.

Tribute must also be paid to the skill or luck whereby the Soviet publicity machine has convinced world opinion that the USSR is gradually evolving towards further liberalization. This widespread and seemingly ineradicable misconception must be worth many an armoured division and clutch of nuclear warheads to the Kremlin – for what foreign state need prepare to defend itself against a régime rolling inexorably forward in the direction of ever greater benignity? Though such episodes as Soviet intervention in Hungary and Czechoslovakia, and the more widely publicized trials of dissident writers, have repeatedly exposed this illusion, perennial optimism about Soviet trends has always reasserted itself.

The space ship
Soyuz 9 on the
launching pad,
1 June 1970.

Besides enjoying all the above advantages, Lenin's heirs have also been very largely protected, through skilful police controls, from such nuisances as industrial strikes, demonstrations against official policy, assassinations of leading statesmen and the pronouncements of permissive-minded clergymen, as well as from hippies, yippies, junkies, sex supermarkets and protesting students. They may therefore congratulate themselves on possessing an administrative, social and political system admirably geared to the needs of government in the space age. Yet they have signally failed to create a society in the remotest degree attractive to those who prize privacy, individual prosperity, the enjoyment of civil rights and freedom from official interference: privileges such as Russians – whether under Muscovite, Imperial or Soviet rule – have seemed ill equipped to grasp, or even to appreciate, throughout the ages. For this, perhaps, historical accident should be blamed – not, certainly, any general lack of talent, energy and courage.

Short Bibliography

BIBLIOGRAPHIES

Grierson, Philip, *Books on Soviet Russia, 1917–1942: a Bibliography and a Guide to Reading* (London, 1943)

Kolarz, Walter, ed., *Books on Communism: a Bibliography* (London, 1963)

Shapiro, David, *A Select Bibliography of Works in English on Russian History, 1801–1917* (Oxford, 1962)

HISTORICAL ATLASES

Adams, Arthur E., Iain M. Matley and William O. McCagg, *An Atlas of Russian and East European History* (London, 1967)

Chew, Allen F., *An Atlas of Russian History: Eleven Centuries of Changing Borders* (London, 1967)

Gilbert, Martin, *Russian History Atlas* (publication pending)

GENERAL WORKS

(a) On the pre-Soviet period (wholly or substantially)

Charques, Richard, *A Short History of Russia* (London, 1956)
The Twilight of Imperial Russia (London, 1958)

Custine, Marquis de, *Russia*, abridged from the French (London, 1855)

Florinsky, Michael T., *Russia: a History and an Interpretation* (2 vols, New York, 1947)
The End of the Russian Empire (New York, 1961)

Freeborn, Richard, *A Short History of Modern Russia* (London, 1966)

Karpovich, Michael, *Imperial Russia, 1801–1917* (New York, 1932)

Kochan, Lionel, *The Making of Modern Russia* (London, 1962)

Mackenzie Wallace, D., *Russia* (3rd ed., 2 vols, London, 1877)

Pares, B., *A History of Russia* (2nd ed., New York, 1928)

Riasanovsky, Nicholas V., *A History of Russia* (New York, 1963)

Seton-Watson, Hugh, *The Decline of Imperial Russia, 1855–1914* (London, 1952)
The Russian Empire, 1801–1917 (Oxford, 1967)

Sumner, B. H., *Survey of Russian History* (London, 1944)

Utechin, S. V., *Everyman's Concise Encyclopaedia of Russia* (London, 1961)

Vernadsky, George, *A History of Russia* (4 vols, New Haven, 1943–59)
A History of Russia (latest rev. ed., New Haven, 1961)

(b) On the Soviet period (wholly or substantially)

Armstrong, John A., *The Politics of Totalitarianism: the Communist Party of the Soviet Union from 1934 to the Present* (New York, 1961)

Carr, E.H., *A History of Soviet Russia: The Bolshevik Revolution, 1917–1923* (3 vols, London, 1952–54); *The Interregnum, 1923–1924* (London, 1954); *Socialism in One Country, 1924–26* (3 vols, London, 1958–64); with R.W. Davies, *Foundations of a Planned Economy, 1926–1929* (2 vols, London, 1969)

Fainsod, Merle, *How Russia is Ruled* (rev. ed., Cambridge, Massachusetts, 1963)

Grey, Ian, *The First Fifty Years: Soviet Russia, 1917–1967* (London, 1967)

McClosky, Herbert, and John E. Turner, *The Soviet Dictatorship* (New York, 1960)

Rauch, Georg von, *A History of Soviet Russia* (5th, rev. ed., New York, 1967)

Seton-Watson, Hugh, *From Lenin to Malenkov: the History of World Communism* (New York, 1953)

Treadgold, Donald W., *Twentieth Century Russia* (2nd ed., Chicago, 1964)

CULTURAL AND INTELLECTUAL HISTORY

Abraham, G., *Studies in Russian Music* (London, 1935)

Billington, James H., *The Icon and the Axe: an Interpretative History of Russian Culture* (London, 1966)

Brown, Edward J., *Russian Literature since the Revolution* (London, 1963)

Calvocoressi, M. D., and G. Abraham, *Masters of Russian Music* (London, 1936)

Carmichael, Joel, *A Cultural History of Russia* (London, 1968)

Gray, Camilla, *The Great Experiment: Russian Art, 1863–1922* (London, 1962)

Hingley, Ronald, *Russian Writers and Society, 1825–1904* (London, 1967)

Kopp, Anatole, *Town and Revolution: Soviet Architecture and City Planning, 1917–1935* (London, 1970)

Mirsky, D. S., *A History of Russian Literature*, ed. and abridged by Francis J. Whitfield (London, 1949)

Olkhovsky, A., *Music under the Soviets* (New York, 1955)

Rice, T. T., *Russian Art* (London, 1949)

Struve, Gleb, *Soviet Russian Literature, 1917–1950* (Norman, Oklahoma, 1951)

Swayze, Harold, *Political Control of Literature in the USSR, 1946–1959* (Cambridge, Massachusetts, 1962)

Utechin, S. V., *Russian Political Thought: a Concise History* (New York, 1964)

REVOLUTIONARY AND COMMUNIST-PARTY HISTORY

Chamberlin, William Henry, *The Russian Revolution, 1917–1921* (2 vols, New York, 1935)

Daniels, Robert Vincent, *Red October: the Bolshevik Revolution of 1917* (London, 1967)

Footman, David, *Red Prelude: a Life of A. I. Zhelyabov* (London, 1944)

Futrell, Michael, *Northern Underground: Episodes of Russian Revolutionary Transport and Communications through Scandinavia and Finland, 1863–1917* (London, 1963)

Hingley, Ronald, *Nihilists: Russian Radicals and Revolutionaries in the Reign of Alexander II, 1855–1881* (London, 1967)
Russian Revolution (London, 1970)

Katkov, George, *Russia 1917: the February Revolution* (London, 1967)

Keep, J. L. H., *The Rise of Social Democracy in Russia* (Oxford, 1963)

Kochan, Lionel, *Russia in Revolution, 1890–1918* (London, 1966)

Lampert, E., *Sons against Fathers: Studies in Russian Radicalism and Revolution* (Oxford, 1965)

Schapiro, Leonard, *The Origin of the Communist Autocracy: Political Opposition in the Soviet State, First Phase, 1917–1922* (London, 1955)
The Communist Party of the Soviet Union (2nd ed., rev. and enlarged, London, 1970)

Schwarz, Solomon M., *The Russian Revolution of 1905: the Workers' Movement and the Formation of Bolshevism and Menshevism* (Chicago, 1967)

Shukman, Harold, *Lenin and the Russian Revolution* (London, 1966)

Ulam, Adam B., *Lenin and the Bolsheviks: the Intellectual and Political History of the Triumph of Communism in Russia* (London, 1965)

Venturi, Franco, *Roots of Revolution: a History of the Populist and Socialist Movements in Nineteenth Century Russia*, trans. from the Italian by Francis Haskell (London, 1960)

Wolfe, Bertram D., *Three who Made a Revolution: a Biographical History* (London, 1956)

Yarmolinsky, Avrahm, *Road to Revolution: a Century of Russian Radicalism* (London, 1957)

BIOGRAPHICAL MATERIAL

(a) *Figures prominent in the pre-Soviet period*

Barbour, Philip L., *Dimitry Called the Pretender: Tsar and Great Prince of All Russia, 1605–1606* (London, 1967)

Fennell, J. L. I., *Ivan the Great of Moscow* (London, 1963)

Grey, Ian, *Ivan the Terrible* (London, 1964)
Peter the Great (London, 1962)
Catherine the Great: Autocrat and Empress of All Russia (London, 1961)
Lang, David Marshall, *The First Russian Radical: Alexander Radishchev, 1749–1802* (London, 1959)
Massie, Robert K., *Nicholas and Alexandra* (London, 1967)
Mosse, W. E., *Alexander II and the Modernization of Russia* (London, 1958)
Oldenbourg, Zoé, *Catherine the Great*, trans. from the French by Anne Carter (London, 1965)
Riasanovsky, Nicholas V., *Nicholas I and Official Nationality in Russia, 1825–55* (Berkeley, 1959)
Sumner, B. H., *Peter the Great and the Emergence of Russia* (London, 1951)

(*b*) *Figures prominent in the Soviet period*

LENIN

Payne, Robert, *The Life and Death of Lenin* (London, 1964)
Schapiro, Leonard, and Peter Reddaway, ed., *Lenin: the Man, the Theorist, the Leader: a Reappraisal* (London, 1967)
Shub, David, *Lenin: a Biography* (London, 1966)

STALIN

Anti-Stalin Campaign and International Communism, The: a Selection of Documents, ed. by the Russian Institute, Columbia University (New York, 1956)
Bialer, Seweryn, ed., *Stalin and his Generals* (London, 1970)
Deutscher, I., *Stalin: a Political Biography* (London, 1967)
Payne, Robert, *The Rise and Fall of Stalin* (London, 1968)
Rigby, T. H., ed., *The Stalin Dictatorship: Khrushchev's 'Secret Speech' and other Documents* (Sydney, 1968)
Smith, Edward Ellis, *The Young Stalin: the Early Years of an Elusive Revolutionary* (London, 1968)

TROTSKY

Deutscher, I., *The Prophet Armed: Trotsky, 1879–1921* (London, 1954)
The Prophet Unarmed: Trotsky, 1921–1929 (London, 1959)
The Prophet Outcast: Trotsky, 1929–1940 (London, 1963)

OTHER DETAILED STUDIES

(*a*) *On the pre-Soviet period (wholly or substantially)*

Blum, Jerome, *Lord and Peasant in Russia: from the Ninth to the Nineteenth Century* (New York, 1964)
Fennell, J. L. I., *The Emergence of Moscow, 1304–1359* (London, 1968)
Greenberg, Louis, *The Jews in Russia: the Struggle for Emancipation* (2 vols in one, New Haven, 1965)
Hingley, Ronald, *The Tsars: Russian Autocrats, 1533–1917* (London, 1968)
The Russian Secret Police: Muscovite, Imperial Russian and Soviet Political Security Operations (London, 1970)
Kennan, George, *Siberia and the Exile System* (2 vols, London, 1891)
Mazour, Anatole G., *The First Russian Revolution, 1825: the Decembrist Movement* (Stanford, 1937)
Robinson, Geroid T., *Rural Russia under the Old Régime* (New York, 1949)
Tupper, Harmon, *To the Great Ocean: Siberia and the Trans-Siberian Railway* (London, 1965)
Walkin, Jacob, *The Rise of Democracy in Pre-revolutionary Russia: Political and Social Institutions under the Last Three Czars* (London, 1963)
Westwood, J. N., *A History of Russian Railways* (London, 1964)

(*b*) *On the Soviet period*

Brzezinski, Zbigniew K., *The Permanent Purge: Politics in Soviet Totalitarianism* (Cambridge, Massachusetts, 1956)
Conquest, Robert, *Power and Policy in the USSR: the Study of Soviet Dynastics* (London, 1961)
The Great Terror: Stalin's Purge of the Thirties (London, 1968)
Justice and the Legal System in the USSR (London, 1968)
The Soviet Police System (London, 1968)
The Nation-Killers: the Soviet Deportation of Nationalities (London, 1970)
Dallin, David J., and Boris I. Nicolaevsky, *Forced Labor in Soviet Russia* (London, 1948)
Daniels, Robert Vincent, *The Conscience of the*

Revolution: Communist Opposition in Soviet Russia (Cambridge, Massachusetts, 1960)

Erickson, John, *The Soviet High Command: a Military-Political History, 1918–1941* (London, 1962)

Fainsod, Merle, *Smolensk under Soviet Rule* (London, 1959)

Fischer, George, *Soviet Opposition to Stalin: a Case Study in World War II* (Cambridge, Massachusetts, 1952)

Footman, David, *Civil War in Russia* (London, 1961)

Katkov, George, *The Trial of Bukharin* (London, 1969)

Kennan, George F., *Russia and the West under Lenin and Stalin* (Boston, 1960)

Kolarz, Walter, *Russia and her Colonies* (London, 1952)

Religion in the Soviet Union (London, 1961)

Leonhard, Wolfgang, *The Kremlin since Stalin*, trans. from the German by Elizabeth Wiske-

mann and Marian Jackson (Oxford, 1962)

Rush, Myron, *The Rise of Khrushchev* (Washington, 1958)

Schwartz, Harry, *Russia's Soviet Economy* (London, 1951)

Seton-Watson, Hugh, *The East European Revolution* (London, 1950)

Swianiewicz, S., *Forced Labour and Economic Development: an Enquiry into the Experience of Soviet Industrialization* (London, 1965)

Tatu, Michel, *Power in the Kremlin: from Khrushchev's Decline to Collective Leadership*, trans. from the French by Helen Katel (London, 1969)

Ulam, Adam B., *Titoism and the Cominform* (Cambridge, Massachusetts, 1952)

Expansion and Co-existence: the History of Soviet Foreign Policy, 1917–67 (London, 1968)

Zawodny, J.K., *Death in the Forest: the Story of the Katyn Forest Massacre* (Notre Dame, 1962)

Alexander's wife, the Empress Elizabeth. Portrait by M. L. E. Vigée-Lebrun. Montpellier Museum, France. *Photo H. Roger Viollet*

99 Building a peasant hut. Etching by J. B. Le Prince (1768). British Museum. *Photo Freeman.*

'Russian Peasants'. Print by J. C. G. Giessler (1798). British Museum. *Photo Freeman.*

100 A St Petersburg merchant and his wife driving in a drozhky. Eighteenth-century engraving. Bibliothèque Nationale, Paris. *Photo H. Roger Viollet.*

101 Russia's first railway, opened in 1837. Engraving of 1838. British Museum. *Photo Freeman.*

102 Manuscripts of works by Alexander Pushkin. State Pushkin Museum, Moscow. *Photo Novosti.*

103 Casting the bronze capital of the Alexander Column. Contemporary lithograph after a drawing by Auguste de Montferrant. Bibliothèque Nationale, Paris. *Photo H. Roger Viollet.*

104-105 Map: the expansion of the Russian Empire in Asia, 1800–1914.

107 View of the palace of 'Mon Plaisir' in the garden at Peterhof. Early nineteenth-century engraving. Victoria and Albert Museum, London. *Photo Freeman.*

108 Michael Speransky. Contemporary portrait. *Photo Novosti.*

109 Alexander I and Napoleon confer on a raft at Tilsit, on the River Niemen. Contemporary engraving. *Photo Mansell Collection.*

110 'La Bataille de la Moscowa' (the Battle of Borodino). Painting by Louis François Le Jeune. Château de Versailles. *Photo Giraudon.*

111 Moscow burns, 1812. Contemporary engraving. British Museum. *Photo Freeman.*

112 The five Decembrist leaders who were hanged in St Petersburg on 13 July 1826. The front page of Herzen's journal *The Polar Star*, published outside Russia *Photo S.C.R.*

113 The public proclamation of the coronation of Nicholas I in Moscow. Lithograph by L. Courtin and V. Adam (1828). Pushkin Fine Arts Museum, Moscow. *Photo Novosti.*

Nicholas I returns to the Palace of Facets, in the Moscow Kremlin, after his coronation. Pushkin Fine Arts Museum, Moscow. *Photo Novosti.*

116 Alexander Pushkin. Portrait by V. A. Tropinin.

Nicholas Gogol. Pencil drawing by Mazer. State Literary Museum, Moscow. *Photo Novosti.*

Michael Lermontov. From a lithograph after a drawing by von Gorbunow. *Photo Mansell Collection.*

117 Alexander Herzen. Photograph by Nadar. *Photo Mansell Collection.*

Ivan Turgenev. Painting by Ilya Repin. Tretyakov Gallery, Moscow. *Photo Novosti.*

Theodore Dostoyevsky. Lithograph based on a photograph of 1865. *Photo Novosti.*

118 'The clemency of the Russian monster'. English cartoon (*c.* 1832). British Museum. *Photo Freeman.*

119 The Emperor Nicholas I. Anonymous painting of 1856 (detail). Collection Lady Zia Wernher. *Photo W. H. Cox.*

120 The British ordnance wharf at Balaclava, 1855. Photograph by Roger Fenton. Gernsheim Collection, University of Texas, Austin.

122 The Emperor Alexander II. *Photo Novosti.*

123 Alexander II's manifesto of 1861, proclaiming the emancipation of the serfs, is read out in public. *Photo Radio Times Hulton Picture Library.*

126 The imperial train is derailed on 19 November 1879. Contemporary artist's impression. *Photo Radio Times Hulton Picture Library.*

127 Michael Loris-Melikov. *Photo Radio Times Hulton Picture Library.*

128 The assassination of Alexander II. Contemporary artist's impression. *Photo Novosti.*

129 The Congress of Berlin, 1878. Contemporary engraving. *Photo Mansell Collection.*

130 'Russian civilization'. Cartoon from the English comic periodical *Judy*, July 1880. British Museum. *Photo Freeman.*

131 The execution of Alexander II's assassins. From an issue of the *Illustrated London News*, 1881. British Museum. *Photo Freeman.*

132 A Jew is beaten during the Kiev pogrom which followed the assassination of Alexander II. Contemporary artist's impression. *Photo Radio Times Hulton Picture Library.*

133 Imperial Russia's social structure derided. Cartoon issued in 1900 by the Union of Russian Socialists. Saltykov-Shchedrin Public Library, Leningrad.

135 Leo Tolstoy. Photograph taken in 1908. *Photo Novosti.*

Anton Chekhov with his wife, Olga Knipper. *Photo Novosti.*

Maxim Gorky, with Constantine Stanislavsky and Mary Lilin. Photograph taken in 1900. *Photo Novosti.*

136 Alexander Borodin. *Photo Mansell Collection.*

Modest Musorgsky. From Modest Musorgsky, *Lettres et Documents* (Moscow, 1932).

Nicholas Rimsky-Korsakov. *Photo Novosti.*

Peter Tchaikovsky with two singers. *Photo Novosti.*

137 A hundred-rouble note, issued in 1898. Collection Thomas. *Photo H. Roger Viollet.*

138 Russian peasant immigrants in Siberia. Convicts working in the mines. Engravings from E. Ukhtomsky, *Travels in the East of Nicholas II, Emperor of Russia* (London, 1896). British Museum. *Photo Freeman.*

139 The Emperor Alexander III with his family. Collection Lady Zia Wernher. *Photo W. H. Cox.*

140 Cartoon celebrating the assassination of V. K. Pleve. From the cover of the French periodical *Burin satirique*, No. 27 (1904). *Photo Radio Times Hulton Picture Library.*

Front page of the revolutionary weekly *Zritel* ('Observer'), St Petersburg (1905).

141 The 'protective' Russian attitude towards Korean victims of the Japanese. Cartoon on a postcard of the Russo-Japanese War period. British Museum.

142 Russians reading news sheets in the Moscow fruit market, September 1905. *Photo Radio Times Hulton Picture Library.*

143 Cossack troops at the Baku oil-wells, 1905. *Photo Novosti.*

Workers outside the Putilov iron and steel works in St Petersburg, January 1905. *Photo Novosti.*

144 A procession in Warsaw in response to the Emperor's manifesto of 17 October 1905. *Photo Mansell Collection.*

145 The Emperor opens the first session of the First State Duma in the Winter Palace, St Petersburg, 27 April 1906. *Photo Radio Times Hulton Picture Library.*

146 A student agitator harangues a group of peasants during the 1905 Revolution. Contemporary artist's impression. *Photo Mansell Collection.*

147 The Emperor's manifesto of 17 October 1905 ridiculed. Two cartoons of late 1905.

148 President Poincaré and the Emperor Nicholas II on the yacht *Standard*, July 1914. *Photo Novosti.*

THE ROMANOV DYNASTY

Theodore Romanov (Philaret)

Michael (1613–45)

Mary Miloslavsky = Alexis (1645–76) = Natalia Naryshkin

THE FIRST MUSCOVITE DYNASTY

Theodore III (1676–82)

Alexander Nevsky

Daniel (1276–1304)

Ivan V (1682–96) Eudoxia Lopukhin = Peter I, the Great = Catherine I (1682–1725) (1725–27)

Yury (1304–25)   Ivan I (1325–41)

Catherine of Mecklenburg

Alexis

Simeon (1341–53) Ivan II (1353–59)

Anne Leopoldovna of Brunswick

Peter II (1727–30)

Anne (1730–40)

Dmitry Donskoy (1359–89)

Ivan VI (1740–41)

Anne of Holstein   Elizabeth (1741–61)

Vasily I (1389–1425)

Vasily II (1425–62)

Peter III = Catherine II, the Great (1762–96) (1761–62)

Ivan III, the Great (1462–1505)

Vasily III (1505–33)

Paul (1796–1801)

Ivan IV, the Terrible (1533–84)

Alexander I (1801–25)

Nicholas I (1825–55)

220 Theodore I (1584–98)

Alexander II (1855–81)

Alexander III (1881–94)

Nicholas II (1894–1917)

Index